LAMDA
FIRST FOLIO
SPEECHES FOR MEN

LAMDA
FIRST FOLIO
SPEECHES FOR MEN

Chosen by Patrick Tucker

PUBLISHED BY
OBERON BOOKS
FOR THE LONDON ACADEMY OF
MUSIC AND DRAMATIC ART

First published in 1997 for LAMDA Ltd.
by Oberon Books Ltd.
(incorporating Absolute Classics)
521 Caledonian Road, London N7 9RH
Tel: 020 7607 3637 / Fax: 020 7607 3629
e-mail: oberon.books@btinternet.com
www.oberonbooks.com

Reprinted with corrections in 2004.

A catalogue record for this book is available from the British Library.

ISBN 1 84002 419 4

Cover design: Society

Cover photograph: John Haynes

Printed in Great Britain by Antony Rowe Ltd, Chippenham.

Foreword

This Volume of seventy one pieces is a companion to *First Folio Speeches for Women*.

Between them, they present many speeches from *The First Folio of Shakespeare*, with notes relating to their performance.

The pieces have been chosen to be suitable for auditions, and for use in the classroom.

Biographies

The Notes on the Speeches have been prepared by Patrick Tucker and Christine Ozanne, who together do the verse work for the Original Shakespeare Company's productions.

Original Shakespeare Company

The Original Shakespeare Company was founded in 1991, and presents plays with professional actors in the Elizabethan manner of no director and no rehearsals, with the actors only working in this way, between 1991 and 2000 the OSC put on over 60 presentations, 29 of which were full length plays, in 5 different countries. The OSC presentations at Shakespeare's Globe in London were *As you Like It* (1997); *King John* (1998); and *Cymbeline* (1999).

Patrick Tucker

Since his first professional production in 1968, he has directed over 200 plays in all forms of theatre, from weekly repertory to the Royal Shakespeare Company. He has also directed more than 150 television dramas ranging from plays for the BBC to many episodes of Liverpool's own soap opera *Brookside*, as well as a feature film *In the Dark.*

He has served on the Artistic Directorate of Shakespeare's Globe since it was formed, and he lectures and teaches these ways of working on Shakespeare all over the world.

He has published a book all about the experiences and lessons learned from working with the Original Shakespeare Company, *Secrets of Acting Shakespeare – The Original Approach*, published by Routledge in 2002. They have also brought out the Second Edition of his earlier *Secrets of Screen Acting.*

He also co-edits *The Shakespeare's Globe Acting Edition* of the plays which presents, in separate volumes, the complete Folio text of the play in modern typeface, together with the full set of Cue Scripts for each part. Twenty-two individual plays are now available from:

M.H. Publications: 020 8455 4640.

Christine Ozanne

Together with her partner, Patrick Tucker, she has been at the forefront of all the Original Shakespeare Company's productions to date, appearing on stage as the Book-Holder (prompter) breaking with this tradition at the Jerash Festival, Jordan 1997, where she appeared as First Fairy and Starveling in *A Midsommer Nights Dreame*, and Lady Capulet in *Romeo and Juliet* in 1999. She has 'verse-nursed' all the performers in these presentations.

She was awarded an Honours Diploma from the Royal Academy of Dramatic Art in 1958 and has worked as an actress and singer in all areas of the profession, repertory and West End theatre, television plays and situation comedies, and numerous commercials.

After becoming involved with the OSC's techniques, she has given many lectures and workshops in the UK, USA, Canada and Australia, with both professional and amateur actors, teachers and students at drama schools including the London Academy of Music and Dramatic Art.

Christine is collaborating with Patrick on a new book to help actors called *The Actor's Survival Handbook,* also published by Routledge in New York.

Contents

10

12

Introduction

This book of speeches is different from any other, in that all the text used is from The First Folio of Shakespeare, and uses the original spelling, punctuation and line arrangements found there.

This is done because I believe that the Folio text includes, in its original form, particular acting clues that help all actors, directors, teachers and general readers, to understand more of what Shakespeare was getting at, and enables anyone to approach a speech without a long and tedious discussion of what the speech is about, what is going on around the speech, or what you the performer would do if you were in the supposed circumstances of the speech.

I shall show that the 1623 First Folio is an immediately accessible tool to the works of William Shakespeare – and is of contemporary relevance to modern actors, readers and scholars.

The claim that the original Folio punctuation and capitalization is a representation of what the actors said all those years ago is challenged by those who maintain that such matters were left to the whim of the individual type setter at the printers. They assert that the Folio details have no authority beyond the fact that the type setters were contemporaries of the actors whose spoken lines they were setting.

My observation is that *all* the Shakespeare pieces I have worked on over the years – whether they are in full length productions, in selected scenes, or in individual speeches – come over better, and are easier to act, when the original text and all its punctuation and capitals are strictly adhered to.

It is because of these results that they are highlighted in the Notes on the Speeches. It also must be mentioned that once some things are 'edited' to be more 'correct', then the flood gates are opened and literally thousands of changes are foisted upon Shakespeare's priceless Folio lines.

Elizabethan Acting

The Elizabethan actors who first performed the plays of Shakespeare worked a very heavy schedule, usually presenting six different full length plays every week – and introducing a new play into the repertoire at two weekly intervals. There was no director in the modern sense, and often the actor had no access to the complete script of the play, but was only given his Cue Script – that is, all the speeches that his character spoke, with just a few words at the start of each speech – his cue words.

My researches show that with this weight of work, there was no time for rehearsal in the sense that we understand the word today, and that the actors must have had a quick and reliable way of approaching a text that allowed them to perform as quickly as we know they did.

I believe that they worked from Shakespeare's text the way an orchestral musician works from a score – they too are not given the complete work, but are given their own notes, and they work from the clues in the music – not just the notes but the notations and added instructions in the scoring. William Shakespeare, an actor himself, would know better than anyone the problems of working to such a tight schedule, and I am sure that he wrote into each speech all the information that modern actors think they need to get from rehearsal – information on mood, attitude and character.

In the speeches that follow, I have written down a few Notes to point the actor in such directions as I feel Shakespeare has outlined – but they are not the sole clues to be got from the text, just the most obvious ones for each speech.

At the end, I have included an Acting Check List – an approach to acting First Folio text; a list of the main clues and how to interpret them.

Introduction to the First Folio

Read the Introduction to the First Folio – reprinted on page 18 – which talks of 'cur'd, and perfect of their limbes', and is signed by those who prepared it – two of Shakespeare's fellow actors and share holders John Heminge and Henrie Condell. They edited these works, and it is important to consider who they were, and what their point of view was, to discover the context of the works as printed in 1623.

All edited versions of Shakespeare – which make upwards of 2000 changes per play from the original – suffer from being treated as pieces of literature, and from being changed accordingly. The works of Shakespeare were written – and should be treated – as pieces of theatre. Reading them with that in mind reveals a whole host of ideas and points of view relevant to any modern performance or reading.

Although they say 'worthie to have bene wish'd, that the Author himselfe had liv'd to have set forth, and overseen his owne writings;' – it is probably fortunate that Shakespeare himself did *not* prepare his own works for publication, and maybe change his works to be more like 'literature', the way Ben Jonson did when he prepared his own Collected Works.

I often direct dramas for television as well as for theatre. Most theatre scripts are published, and are as accessible to the general reader as they are to me, but television scripts are only intended to be read by those who must interpret them – the actors, director, prop buyers, camera personnel etc. So the layout and terms used sometimes only make sense to the actual practitioners of preparing drama for the screen.

I believe the same is true of all the written work of William Shakespeare – the layout and terms used are specifically for his co-workers, and not necessarily immediately apparent to the general reader. Remember, the plays of Shakespeare were put on by a busy company, used to presenting six different plays a week. Under this sort of heavy schedule, Shakespeare himself would have worked into the scripts – spelled and punctuated the way they did then – those vital clues as to how to act and present each speech, and these elements would have been retained by the two fellow actors who prepared his works for publication as a commemorate to him.

That is why in this book of speeches I have used only the First Folio text, and start off by giving an approach to First Folio text, that includes those clues that modern performers of Shakespeare can use to let the original language augment the directing and interpretation. A fuller explanation of what each section means will be found in the General Notes to the Actor, following.

Patrick Tucker
London 1997

Heminge and Condell

The Introduction To The First Folio 1623

To the great Variety of Readers:

From the most able, to him that can but spell: There you are number'd. We had rather you were weighd. Especially, when the fate of all Bookes depends upon your capacities: and not of your heads alone, but of your purses. Well! It is now publique, and you wil stand for your priviledges wee know: to read, and censure. Do so, but buy it first. That doth best commend a Booke, the Stationer saies. Then, how odde soever your braines be, or your wisedomes, make your licence the same, and spare not. Judge your sixe-pen'orth, your shillings worth, your five shillings worth at a time, or higher, so you rise to the just rates, and welcome. But, what ever you do, Buy. Censure will not drive a Trade, or make the Jacke go. And though you be a Magistrate of wit, and sit on the Stage at *Black-Friers*, or the *Cock-pit*, to arraigne Playes dailie, know, these Playes have had their triall alreadie, and stood out all Appeales; and do now come forth quitted rather by a Decree of Court, then any purchas'd Letters of commendation.

It had bene a thing, we confesse, worthie to have bene wished, that the Author himselfe had liv'd to have set forth, and overseen his owne writings; But since it hath bin ordain'd otherwise, and he by death departed from that right, we pray you do not envie his Friends, the office of their care, and paine, to have collected and publish'd them; and so to have publish'd them, as where (before) you were abus'd with diverse stolne, and surreptitious copies, maimed, and deformed by the frauds and stealthes of injurious impostors, that expos'd them: even those, are now offer'd to your view cur'd, and perfect of their limbes; and all the rest, absolute in their numbers, as he conceived them. Who, as he was a happie imitator of Nature, was a most gentle expresser of it. His mind and hand went together: And what he thought, he uttered with that easinesse, that wee have scarse received from him a blot in his papers. But it is not our province, who onely gather his works, and give them you, to praise him. It is yours that reade him. And there we hope, to your divers capacities, you will finde enough, both to draw, and hold you: for his wit can no more lie hid, then it could be lost. Reade him, therefore; and againe, and againe: And if then you doe not like him, surely you are in some manifest danger, not to understand him. And so we leave you to other of his Friends, whom if you need, can bee your guides: if you neede them not, you can leade your selves, and others.

And such Readers we wish him.

John Heminge
Henrie Condell

General Notes to the Actor on performing the Speeches

The numbers correspond to the Note Numbers at the end of each speech, under 'First Folio Verse Notes'.

NOTE 1: POETRY/PROSE

If every line begins with a capital letter it is poetry or verse; if the text runs on in a jumbled up fashion – it is prose. Poetry is 'heightened' language and your character is choosing to speak that way. By 'choosing' the end word of the line you automatically put the text into a metered pattern. (See also Notes 9 and 26.)

Prose is more relaxed speech and needs to be a contrast (theatrically) to poetry. Many characters speak both prose and poetry, which is a *big* clue for a gear change between the two.

Shakespeare often marked the major changes in a character by the moment they change from mostly speaking in one form, to speaking in the other.

NOTE 2: LONG THOUGHTS

Many of the speeches contain much longer thoughts than we expect. Modern editors have a tendency to break speeches up into bite sized chunks, but as a piece of theatre they play much better in their original long length. Keep the thought going until the full stop (but you can *breathe* without the thought stopping). The full stop (or question mark/ exclamation point if the next word is capitalized) is the end of a thought – no matter how long or short that thought may be. If you highlight the last few words before a full stop, it will not only show you how long a thought you are embarking upon, but will give a hint as to what the whole thought is about. Find a way to keep the thought going through commas, colons and semi-colons, finally ending the thought only at the full stop. (See also Note 18.)

NOTE 3: COLONS AND SEMI-COLONS

The colon often stands for the word 'therefore' or 'because'. It is a way of joining up different parts of a long thought, so that the next part of the thought is related to the previous one. A semi-colon stands for the word 'and', and means that the next bit of the thought joins on to the previous bit. The important thing is *never* to treat them as full stops or periods.

Sometimes, a colon can indicate an unfinished thought, or where the thought gets broken. It is always an interesting acting note to come across one, and something should be done about it.

Technically speaking, a complete thought is a compound sentence whose different clauses are joined together by colons and semi-colons.

NOTE 4: SURPRISES AND UNEXPECTED PUNCTUATION

An audience can often see where an idea or a speech (or a character) is going. If they, the audience, get there before the performer does, then that is theatrical boredom. Shakespeare being the supreme theatrical writer, often takes the character in a completely unexpected direction during a speech – for instance, not building to the end, but building to three quarters of the way, and then undercutting. This makes the audience follow closely, for they cannot anticipate what will happen next.

The problem for the actor is that just as Shakespeare surprises an audience, he can sometimes surprise you the performer – be aware of surprising gear changes – and fulfil them.

NOTE 5: CAPITALS AND ITALICS

In verse, the first letter of each line is a Capital. Do not ignore the apparently random Capitalised words in the rest of the line. They are carefully chosen to give an actor's scoring for the whole speech. By giving them an extra 'choice' they are like stepping stones through the speech. (See also Note 26.) Words in Italics are either words of songs, foreign words or proper names.

NOTE 6: SPELLING AND PRONUNCIATION

The original spelling was phonetic. They also had many words with an extra 'e', such as heare, keepe, selfe, soule, againe, naile, walles, ribbes, which are to be pronounced the way they are today.

Where the same word is printed either with or without an extra 'e', then that is an indication of an extra choice or stress on that word. This means that the word 'mee' is *not* the same as 'me' – it is an additional piece of information to the actor as to how to perform it.

NOTE 7: ' ED' AND ' 'D'

Words ending with '-ed' or '-'d' are clearly printed according to the required meter, and to keep it they are pronounced either as ED (blessed sounding blessèd), or as 'D (bless'd sounding blest).

Example:

> My Leige, I am advis<u>ed</u> what I say,
> Neither disturb<u>ed</u> with the effect of Wine,
> Nor headie-rash provoak<u>'d</u> with raging ire,
> Albeit my wrongs might make one wiser mad.

NOTE 8: ALTERNATIVE SPELLING

'than' was usually printed as 'then'. 'show' as 'shew'. 'I'
can be either the first person singular or 'Aye' (as in 'yes')
and Ile = I'll; do's = does and doe = do.

In the Folio they sometimes use abbreviations, so L.
stands for Lord, S. for Saint – but M. could be either Mister,
Master or Monsieur.

NOTE 9: MASCULINE AND FEMININE ENDINGS
(AND ALEXANDRINES)

Masculine = 10 bits or 5 DI DUMs (the line ending DI
DUM). You choose the end word. This is particularly
important where the end word is one normally unstressed, or
where the punctuation leads you to think about running one
line into the next (enjambing). *Do not do this* – Shakespeare
puts the end word there precisely to inform you and the
audience of a particular meaning. If he had wanted the lines
to run on to each other, he would have written them that
way.

Feminine = 11 bits (line ending DI DUM DI), where the
end word is weakened. If the last word is more than one
syllable, the choice could go to the next to last syllable. If
the last word is one syllable, the choice could go to the next
to last word.

Shakespeare started his writing using masculine
endings, but as his style developed, he started using more
feminine endings, using the device to vary the lines and
make them more organic. This does not affect the actor –
if there is a masculine ending – choose the end word, if it
is a feminine ending, then the acting note to you is that the
final word is weakened, and you must make that a
character choice.

If the line adds up to 12 bits, this is called an Alexandrine
and the line is overloaded. The delivery can therefore have

a squeezed or constipated delivery – you are trying to squeeze more thoughts into the line than the line can hold.

NOTE 10: ALLITERATION AND ASSONANCE

Alliteration is where the consonants are the same = 'be made more miserable'.

Assonance is where the vowel sounds are the same = 'any liquid thing you will'. These are additional ways for the author to bring certain words to your notice, of encouraging you to give them a little extra choice. You must create the character who *wants* to use those alliterations, and make those assonances.

NOTE 11: RHYMING COUPLETS

Some speeches are made up entirely of rhyming couplets; more often they will come at the end of a speech. Always acknowledge them by positively making them rhyme. The audience will be hearing the rhymes, and if you do not make them part of your acting choices, they will seem to be unmotivated, and therefore a lie.

A rhyming couplet at an exit is a wonderful thing – by really hitting it, it is like a trampoline that bounces you off the stage with panache.

NOTE 12: SINGLE 'O'

The single 'O' is not quite the same as 'oh'. 'O' is more like an emotion or exclamation, and can be expressed as a sound. The volume or pitch of the sound is entirely up to you. Most actors swallow their 'O's', as if they wish they were not there. Go for them!

NOTE 13: REPEATED WORDS

It is totally unnatural to 'just repeat' words without a good reason. So long as you say the second word (or words) differently to the first and your character justifies the reason for doing so, it will appear perfectly natural.

For example, with Lady Anne in *Richard III* – 'Set downe, set downe your honourable load' – say the second 'set downe' louder than the first, and the reason will be obvious – that is, her attendants did not hear her the first time!

NOTE 14: LISTS

If your speech contains a list (of any kind), always look carefully at the order of the list since Shakespeare deliberately puts things in an unusual sequence which can surprise you and your audience. Do not assume things build to a climax. Lists and whole speeches often peak before the end.

An 'illogical' list (such as Kate has in her final speech of *The Taming of the Shrew*: 'Lord/King/ Governour'), might mean that the character is not as sincere as you thought.

NOTE 15: DOUBLE ENTENDRES

The Elizabethans were more honest about enjoying bawdy references than some of us are today, and a lot more of Shakespeare's words have bawdy double meanings than we now realise. A double entendre is just that, a *double* meaning – it should not be played as a *single* entendre.

It is not essential that the audience understand every Elizabethan sexual innuendo, but it is important that the knowledge that you are using a double entendre informs your attitude and mood – so if in doubt, twinkle a lot.

NOTE 16: BRACKETS

There are many reasons why certain words are put into brackets – and the main acting note is simple: just say them differently. This can include talking to the audience, talking aside to a different character; muttering the words etc. etc.

Brackets do not always imply that what is enclosed is an aside or a throw-away line; they can have the same effect as having the enclosed words printed in bold.

NOTE 17: HALF-LINES, AND ODD-LENGTH LINES

If you find a half-line in the middle of a straight run of regular verse, then the indication is that there is a pause required for 'business' or 'effect'. You may indeed find two half-lines which is a positive 'pause' clue. The implication is simple: since Shakespeare knows how to give you a pause (an unfulfilled half line), if he does not give you such a clue – do not pause, but get on with it.

An odd-length line (such as with only 8 bits instead of 10), means that there is a pause somewhere around – and the actor decides where in the line the pause should be.

An odd-length of more than 10 is either a feminine ending, an Alexandrine, just occasionally an Alexandrine with a feminine ending, or might even be an oasis of prose. (See also Notes 1 and 9.) Because it is not standard, it should not be acted as if it were. (For example, a line with only 9 bits could be seen as syncopated, with the missing beat showing where the pause is.)

Example (Viola:)

That me thought her eyes had lost her tongue,

could be spoken:

That   me thought her eyes had lost her tongue,

If the speech begins with a half-line, this does not indicate a pause to start with, but probably that this line finishes off a half-line that the previous speaker ended with – and so is in fact a clue to come quickly in on cue.

NOTE 18: MID-LINE ENDINGS

If the full stop comes at the end of a full line (but still in the middle of a speech) then a fractional pause is needed to think of your next new thought. If, however, the full stop comes in the middle of a line, you must finish the thought, but start the new thought immediately without pausing or breathing in order to keep the meter going. In other words – the new thought is already in your mind before finishing the old one. This technique produces a wonderful force to the character, and if you have several mid-line endings in one speech, it can have a really powerful impact and drive.

Sometimes (if it is followed by a Capital letter) an exclamation mark or question mark is also a mid-line ending.

A mid-line ending is like a charge of adrenalin, often meaning that you do not want the other character to interrupt you (as if they are about to draw breath to speak) – so get on with it.

NOTE 19: DIFFERENT RHYTHMS

Christopher Marlowe was the first major playwright to experiment with changing rhythms as an additional way of communicating with the performer. Look how the rhythm changes in the third line of Faustus' passion over Helen of Troy:

> Was this the face that launch'd a thousand ships?
> And burnt the topless towers of Ilium?
> Sweet Helen, make me immortal with a kiss.

Shakespeare took this idea, and developed it into a powerful device of changing rhythms feeding changing thoughts and attitudes.

If the whole speech is not in iambic pentameters (5 lots of DI DUM), but in something different (such as 4 lots of DI DUM), then do it differently – sing it, dance it, what you will, but do not speak it as if it were the usual rhythm.

NOTE 20: SEPARATIONS

Where one word ends and the next word begins with the same consonant – always separate them: i.e. glorious Summer; Yorke claims; of Vertuous etc. This gives a little extra choice to the second word – and it is a choice that the author intended.

NOTE 21: COMPLEX/SIMPLE

Most verse lines in Shakespeare contain the verbal 'conceits' outlined in these notes, and should be observed and acted upon to gain full advantage when acting it out. The author, however, was perfectly capable of writing simple lines or phrases, which, when said 'simply' are greatly effective.

Examples:

Viola: What Country (friends) is this?

Lysander: How now, my love; why is your cheek so pale?

Lady Macbeth: Give me the daggers.

Cymbeline's Queene: Now Master Doctor, have you brought those drugges?

If you try to smear emotion on to a simple line it becomes untrue or sounds 'Shakespearean' in the wrong sense of the word! Someone expressing themselves with wit and double entendres, with metaphors and clever words, is someone struggling to express a complex feeling.

The gear change in a speech or character in switching between complex and simple language is always a wonderful acting clue.

NOTE 22: TITLES

If your character addresses someone in different ways, then the way they are said is not the same! For example, with Madam, Mistris, Lady, Cousin, Majesty, Your Grace, My Lord, Sir, My Liege etc. each requires a different attitude or gesture, whether formal or familiar, respectful or grovelling, etc.

Take particular notice of 'you' and 'thee'. They are not the same. You/your is more formal or public; thee/thou more intimate or personal. Sometimes you will change between the two within one speech. Try to physicalize the difference for the greatest theatrical effect (one way is to get closer for a 'thee', be more distant for a 'you').

NOTE 23: REPETITION OF A CLUE

Sometimes a particular clue (some alliteration; a mid-line ending; some bawdy reference) is repeated and done many times in one speech. This is in itself a clue – it is a large clue, and a large clue needs a larger theatricalization than a small one!

NOTE 24: ILLUSTRATING

Shakespeare was quite clear as to what an actor was required to do, as in Hamlet's advice to the Players: 'Sute the Action to the Word, the Word to the Action' – in other words, illustrate.

Many modern acting teachers tell their students not to illustrate – so you can experiment with either following them, or trying out Shakespeare's acting instructions, and see which gets you the best results.

NOTE 25: SOLILOQUY

A Soliloquy suffers from modern attitudes of 'talking to oneself', or even of 'talking to the invisible man'. In Shakespeare's day-lit theatre, this concept was beyond them, and a Soliloquy was when the character talked to the audience.

It is important to realise that there is no rule that the sense is the 'innermost thoughts' of the character – characters can lie or tell the truth to the audience in the same way that they do to each other. A complex Soliloquy, packed with double meanings and verbal conceits, is hardly a person sincerely telling the audience what they are really thinking.

When talking to the audience, do not talk over their heads, or to the back wall, but make proper eye to eye contact with many people in turn, and see how it will galvanise the whole audience.

NOTE 26: CHOOSING WORDS

When we say 'choose' certain words; as in 'choose the end word' or 'choose the capitalised words' or 'choose the second, because you said the first', it is up to the actor as to how they choose. In other words, don't think you have to stress or emphasise; you can 'choose' with de-emphasis, with pitch, pace, tone, volume etc.

The way of choosing is yours, the performer; the genius nudging you to choose is Shakespeare's.

The Speeches

ARRANGEMENT:

The speeches are arranged in the main categories of Comedies, Tragedies, Romances and Histories, and then alphabetically by play (the Histories are in chronological order), and in the order in which the speech occurs in that particular play.

There is an Index at the end both of the first line, and where appropriate of the most famous line in the speech.

As you Like it, II-1

DUKE SENIOR

Now my Coe-mates, and brothers in exile:
Hath not old custome made this life more sweete
Then that of painted pompe?   Are not these woods
More free from perill then the envious Court?
Heere feele we not the penaltie of *Adam*,
The seasons difference, as the Icie phange
And churlish chiding of the winters winde,
Which when it bites and blowes upon my body
Even till I shrinke with cold, I smile, and say
This is no flattery: these are counsellors
That feelingly perswade me what I am:
Sweet are the uses of adversitie
Which like the toad, ougly and venemous,
Weares yet a precious Jewell in his head:
And this our life exempt from publike haunt,
Findes tongues in trees, bookes in the running brookes,
Sermons in stones, and good in every thing.

FIRST FOLIO VERSE NOTES:

Look at the particular words in capitals – 'Coe-mates/
Court/Icie/Jewell': **See Note 5**.

In line 5, notice the long spelling of 'Heere': **See Note 6**.

From line 3 it is one thought to the end: **See Note 2**.

There is a lot of good alliteration and assonance: **See Note 10**.

The colons are part of the argument: **See Note 3**.

The final build is of linked words: 'tongues' with 'trees';
'bookes' with 'brookes' so we would expect a word
beginning with 'g' to go with 'good' – but we don't get one:
See Note 4.

As you Like it, II-7

JAQUES

All the world's a stage,
And all the men and women, meerely Players;
They have their *Exits* and their Entrances,
And one man in his time playes many parts,
His Acts being seven ages. At first the Infant,
Mewling, and puking in the Nurses armes:
Then, the whining Schoole-boy with his Satchell
And shining morning face, creeping like snaile
Unwillingly to schoole. And then the Lover,
Sighing like Furnace, with a wofull ballad
Made to his Mistresse eye-brow. Then, a Soldier,
Full of strange oaths, and bearded like the Pard,
Jelous in honor, sodaine, and quicke in quarrell,
Seeking the bubble Reputation
Even in the Canons mouth: And then, the Justice
In faire round belly, with good Capon lin'd,
With eyes severe, and beard of formall cut,
Full of wise sawes, and moderne instances,
And so he playes his part. The sixt age shifts
Into the leane and slipper'd Pantaloone,
With spectacles on nose, and pouch on side,
His youthfull hose well sav'd, a world too wide,
For his shrunke shanke, and his bigge manly voice,
Turning againe toward childish trebble pipes,
And whistles in his sound. Last Scene of all,
That ends this strange eventfull historie,
Is second childishnesse, and meere oblivion,
Sans teeth, sans eyes, sans taste, sans every thing.

FIRST FOLIO VERSE NOTES:

The speech starts with a half-line: **See Note 17**; and the first 5 lines are all one thought, ending in the middle of a line: **See Notes 2 & 18**.

Line 2 has a feminine ending: **See Note 9**; and there are a lot of mid-line endings, keeping a drive in the argument: **See Note 18**, especially when it introduces the description of the next 'age'.

The spelling of 'meerely' suggests an attitude: **See Note 6**.

There are many capitalized words: **See Note 5**; and, in the last line, notice that it is the word 'sans' which is repeated 4 times: **See Note 13**.

The Comedie of Errors, V-1

ANTIPHOLUS OF EPHESUS

My Liege, I am advised what I say,
Neither disturbed with the effect of Wine,
Nor headie-rash provoak'd with raging ire,
Albeit my wrongs might make one wiser mad.
This woman lock'd me out this day from dinner;
That Goldsmith there, were he not pack'd with her,
Could witnesse it: for he was with me then,
Who parted with me to go fetch a Chaine,
Promising to bring it to the Porpentine,
Where *Balthasar* and I did dine together.
Our dinner done, and he not comming thither,
I went to seeke him. In the street I met him,
And in his companie that Gentleman.
There did this perjur'd Goldsmith sweare me downe,
That I this day of him receiv'd the Chaine,
Which God he knowes, I saw not. For the which,
He did arrest me with an Officer.
I did obey, and sent my Pesant home
For certaine Duckets: he with none return'd.
Then fairely I bespoke the Officer
To go in person with me to my house.
By'th'way, we met my wife, her sister, and a rabble more
Of vilde Confederates: Along with them
They brought one *Pinch*, a hungry leane-fac'd Villaine;
A meere Anatomie, a Mountebanke,
A thred-bare Jugler, and a Fortune-teller,
A needy-hollow-ey'd-sharpe-looking-wretch;
A living dead man. This pernicious slave,
Forsooth tooke on him as a Conjurer:
And gazing in mine eyes, feeling my pulse,
And with no-face (as 'twere) out-facing me,
Cries out, I was possest. Then altogether

They fell upon me, bound me, bore me thence,
And in a darke and dankish vault at home
There left me and my man, both bound together,
Till gnawing with my teeth my bonds in sunder,
I gain'd my freedome; and immediately
Ran hether to your Grace, whom I beseech
To give me ample satisfaction
For these deepe shames, and great indignities.

FIRST FOLIO VERSE NOTES:

Lines 1 to 4 are one thought, and the next 6 lines are also only one thought: **See Note 2**. The argument is made clearer by observing the colons and semi-colons: **See Note 3**.

This speech, unusually, has a lot of very short thoughts.

The '-ed' endings are needed to keep the meter, such as 'advised' and 'disturbed': **See Note 7**.

The speech starts off addressing the Duke as 'My Liege', but ends with 'your Grace': **See Note 22**.

There are 4 mid-line endings in the speech, all of which drive Antipholus on: **See Note 18**.

The capitalized words are interesting: **See Note 5**; and there are 4 lines that start with the word 'A': **See Note 13**.

Line 22 'By'th'way, we met ...' is very long indeed: **See Note 17**.

Loves Labour's lost, III-1

BEROWNE

O, and I forsooth in love,
I that have beene loves whip?
A verie Beadle to a humerous sigh: A Criticke,
Nay, a night-watch Constable.
A domineering pedant ore the Boy,
Then whom no mortall so magnificent.
This wimpled, whyning, purblinde waiward Boy,
This signior *Junios* gyant dwarfe, don *Cupid*,
Regent of Love-rimes, Lord of folded armes,
Th'annointed soveraigne of sighes and groanes:
Liedge of all loyterers and malecontents:
Dread Prince of Placcats, King of Codpeeces.
Sole Emperator and great generall
Of trotting Parrators (O my little heart.)
And I to be a Corporall of his field,
And weare his colours like a Tumblers hoope.
What? I love, I sue, I seeke a wife,
A woman that is like a Germane Clocke,
Still a repairing: ever out of frame,
And never going a right, being a Watch:
But being watcht, that it may still goe right.
Nay, to be perjurde, which is worst of all:
And among three, to love the worst of all,
A whitly wanton, with a velvet brow.
With two pitch bals stucke in her face for eyes.
I, and by heaven, one that will doe the deede,
Though *Argus* were her Eunuch and her garde.
And I to sigh for her, to watch for her,
To pray for her, go to: it is a plague
That *Cupid* will impose for my neglect,
Of his almighty dreadfull little might.
Well, I will love, write, sigh, pray, shue, grone,
Some men must love my Lady, and some Jone.

FIRST FOLIO VERSE NOTES:

This speech is a soliloquy: **See Note 25**.

It also starts with a nice single 'O': **See Note 12**.

The first 2 lines are half-lines, showing that there is a pause: **See Note 17**.

The repeated word 'I' also assonates with 'wife': **See Notes 10 & 13**.

The punctuation being kept to (as in 'With two pitch bals stucke ...') starting a new thought, makes for a more theatrical presentation: **See Note 4**. This also applies to the end of the next thought: 'and her garde.', with an entirely fresh one starting with 'And I to sigh ...'.

The Folio prints 'Germane Cloake' – this has reluctantly been changed to 'Germane Clocke' because of the sense.

'Junios' = junior.

Measure, For Measure, II-2

ANGELO

From thee: even from thy vertue.
What's this? what's this? is this her fault, or mine?
The Tempter, or the Tempted, who sins most? ha?
Not she: nor doth she tempt: but it is I,
That, lying by the Violet in the Sunne,
Doe as the Carrion do's, not as the flowre,
Corrupt with vertuous season: Can it be,
That Modesty may more betray our Sence
Then womans lightnesse? having waste ground enough,
Shall we desire to raze the Sanctuary
And pitch our evils there? oh fie, fie, fie:
What dost thou? or what art thou *Angelo*?
Dost thou desire her fowly, for those things
That make her good? oh, let her brother live:
Theeves for their robbery have authority,
When Judges steale themselves: what, doe I love her,
That I desire to heare her speake againe?
And feast upon her eyes? what is't I dreame on?
Oh cunning enemy, that to catch a Saint,
With Saints dost bait thy hooke: most dangerous
Is that temptation, that doth goad us on
To sinne, in loving vertue: never could the Strumpet
With all her double vigor, Art, and Nature
Once stir my temper: but this vertuous Maid
Subdues me quite: Ever till now
When men were fond, I smild, and wondred how.

FIRST FOLIO VERSE NOTES:

This is a soliloquy: <u>**See Note 25**</u>.

The first 2 words of line 2 are repeated – there must be a good acting reason for this: <u>**See Note 13**</u>. There must also be a good acting reason for the 13 question marks in the piece: <u>**See Note 23**</u>.

In the 6th line, 'doe' = do, and 'do's' = does: <u>**See Note 8**</u>.

The cleverness of 'Tempter' compared with 'Tempted', which are capitalized: <u>**See Note 5**</u>, and the alliterations of 'I/lying/Violet' add to the interpretation: <u>**See Note 10**</u>.

The last 8 lines are all one thought: <u>**See Note 2**</u>, and the use of the colon helps to understand the argument: <u>**See Note 3**</u>.

The sense of this piece is very much refined by choosing the end words of each line: <u>**See Note 9**</u>.

Measure, For Measure, III-1

DUKE

Be absolute for death: either death or life
Shall thereby be the sweeter.   Reason thus with life:
If I do loose thee, I do loose a thing
That none but fooles would keepe: a breath thou art,
Servile to all the skyie-influences,
That dost this habitation where thou keepst
Hourely afflict: Meerely, thou art deaths foole,
For him thou labourst by thy flight to shun,
And yet runst toward him still.   Thou art not noble,
For all th'accommodations that thou bearst,
Are nurst by basenesse: Thou'rt by no meanes valiant,
For thou dost feare the soft and tender forke
Of a poore worme: thy best of rest is sleepe,
And that thou oft provoakst, yet grosselie fearst
Thy death, which is no more.   Thou art not thy selfe,
For thou exists on manie a thousand graines
That issue out of dust.   Happie thou art not,
For what thou hast not, still thou striv'st to get,
And what thou hast forgetst.   Thou art not certaine,
For thy complexion shifts to strange effects,
After the Moone: If thou art rich, thou'rt poore,
For like an Asse, whose backe with Ingots bowes;
Thou bearst thy heavie riches but a journie,
And death unloads thee; Friend hast thou none.
For thine owne bowels which do call thee, fire
The meere effusion of thy proper loines
Do curse the Gowt, Sapego, and the Rheume
For ending thee no sooner.   Thou hast nor youth, nor age
But as it were an after-dinners sleepe
Dreaming on both, for all thy blessed youth
Becomes as aged, and doth begge the almes
Of palsied-Eld: and when thou art old, and rich
Thou hast neither heate, affection, limbe, nor beautie

To make thy riches pleasant: what's yet in this
That beares the name of life?   Yet in this life
Lie hid moe thousand deaths; yet death we feare
That makes these oddes, all even.

FIRST FOLIO VERSE NOTES:

The first 4 words do not end with a full stop – they are the beginning of an argument, not a statement: **See Note 3**.

The colons and semi-colons throughout the speech help sharpen the argument: **See Note 3**.

The first 5 thoughts have mid-line endings: **See Note 18**, which brings out the one thought that finishes at the end of a line: 'Friend hast thou none.'

There are several shortened words: 'keepst/labourst/runst/ bearst/provoakst/fearst' etc. which suggests a certain speech style: **See Notes 23 & 26**.

The use of 'thou' throughout gives a strange personal intensity to the whole piece: **See Note 22**.

Editors change 'which do call thee, fire' to 'which do call thee, Sire'.

'moe' = more; and 'Eld' = old age: **See Note 8**.

'Sapego' = a disfiguring skin disease.

Measure, For Measure, III-1

CLAUDIO

I, but to die, and go we know not where,
To lie in cold obstruction, and to rot,
This sensible warme motion, to become
A kneaded clod; And the delighted spirit
To bath in fierie floods, or to recide
In thrilling Region of thicke-ribbed Ice,
To be imprison'd in the viewlesse windes
And blowne with restlesse violence round about
The pendant world: or to be worse then worst
Of those, that lawlesse and incertaine thought,
Imagine howling, 'tis too horrible.
The weariest, and most loathed worldly life
That Age, Ache, perjury, and imprisonment
Can lay on nature, is a Paradise
To what we feare of death.

Sweet Sister, let me live.
What sinne you do, to save a brothers life,
Nature dispenses with the deede so farre,
That it becomes a vertue.

FIRST FOLIO VERSE NOTES:

The first word can have the meaning 'Aye': **See Note 6**.

The first 11 lines are all one thought: **See Note 2**; and builds to the phrase ''tis too horrible.'

In line 13 the original word in the Folio 'perjury' is kept over the editor's usual choice of 'penury'.

The list of 'Age, Ache, perjury, and imprisonment' needs acknowledgement: **See Note 14**.

The word 'Paradise' (capitalized: **See Note 5**) alliterates with 'perjury', and the middle of 'imprisonment': **See Note 10**.

The gap near the end is where his sister Isabella interrupts.

The Merchant of Venice, I-3

SHYLOCKE

Signior *Anthonio*, many a time and oft
In the Ryalto you have rated me
About my monies and my usances:
Still have I borne it with a patient shrug,
(For suffrance is the badge of all our Tribe.)
You call me misbeleever, cut-throate dog,
And spet upon my Jewish gaberdine,
And all for use of that which is mine owne.
Well then, it now appeares you neede my helpe:
Goe to then, you come to me, and you say,
Shylocke, we would have moneyes, you say so:
You that did voide your rume upon my beard,
And foote me as you spurne a stranger curre
Over your threshold, moneyes is your suite.
What should I say to you?   Should I not say,
Hath a dog money?   Is it possible
A curre should lend three thousand ducats? or
Shall I bend low, and in a bond-mans key
With bated breath, and whispring humblenesse,
Say this: Faire sir, you spet on me on Wednesday last;
You spurn'd me such a day; another time
You cald me dog: and for these curtesies
Ile lend you thus much moneyes.

FIRST FOLIO VERSE NOTES:

In line 2 there is a double entendre for the word 'rated' – both for the money sense, and in the sense of 'berated': **See Note 15**.

The brackets should be used: **See Note 16**, as should the choice of which word ends a particular line: **See Note 9**; in particular, choosing the word 'or' to end the line 17 gives suspense to what follows.

The mid-line endings give a thrust and urgency to the speech: **See Note 18**, and the colons sort out the argument: **See Note 3**.

The word 'spet' means 'spat' (and may be a pronunciation clue): **See Note 6**.

The Merchant of Venice, III-1

SHYLOCKE

To baite fish withall, if it will feede nothing
else, it will feede my revenge; he hath disgrac'd me, and
hindred me halfe a million, laught at my losses, mockt at
my gaines, scorned my Nation, thwarted my bargaines,
cooled my friends, heated my enemies, and what's the
reason? I am a *Jewe*: Hath not a *Jew* eyes? hath not a
Jew hands, organs, dementions, sences, affections, passi-
ons, fed with the same foode, hurt with the same wea-
pons, subject to the same diseases, healed by the same
meanes, warmed and cooled by the same Winter and
Sommer as a Christian is: if you pricke us doe we not
bleede? if you tickle us, doe we not laugh? if you poison
us doe we not die? and if you wrong us shall we not revenge? if we are like you in the rest, we will resemble you
in that. If a *Jew* wrong a *Christian*, what is his humility,
revenge? If a *Christian* wrong a *Jew*, what should his suf-
ferance be by Christian example, why revenge? The villanie you teach me I will execute, and it shall goe hard
but I will better the instruction.

FIRST FOLIO VERSE NOTES:

The whole speech is in prose: **See Note 1**; but the thoughts must still be guided by the punctuation; in particular, 'I am a Jewe' is not a statement ending in a full stop, but the beginning of an argument, and so ends with a colon: **See Note 3**.

There are question marks, and they should all be played *as* questions.

There are a number of lists, all of which need careful judgement: **See Note 14**.

It is the word 'same' that is repeated 5 times: **See Note 13**.

The Merchant of Venice, III-2

BASSANIO

So may the outward showes be least themselves
The world is still deceiv'd with ornament.
In Law, what Plea so tanted and corrupt,
But being season'd with a gracious voice,
Obscures the show of evill? In Religion,
What damned error, but some sober brow
Will blesse it, and approve it with a text,
Hiding the grosenesse with faire ornament:
There is no voice so simple, but assumes
Some marke of vertue on his outward parts;
How manie cowards, whose hearts are all as false
As stayers of sand, weare yet upon their chins
The beards of *Hercules* and frowning *Mars*,
Who inward searcht, have lyvers white as milke,
And these assume but valors excrement,
To render them redoubted. Looke on beautie,
And you shall see 'tis purchast by the weight,
Which therein workes a miracle in nature,
Making them lightest that weare most of it:
So are those crisped snakie golden locks
Which makes such wanton gambols with the winde
Upon supposed fairenesse, often knowne
To be the dowrie of a second head,
The scull that bred them in the Sepulcher.
Thus ornament is but the guiled shore
To a most dangerous sea: the beautious scarfe
Vailing an Indian beautie; In a word,
The seeming truth which cunning times put on
To intrap the wisest. Therefore then thou gaudie gold,
Hard food for *Midas*, I will none of thee,
Nor none of thee thou pale and common drudge
'Tweene man and man: but thou, thou meager lead

Which rather threatnest then dost promise ought,
Thy palenesse moves me more then eloquence,
And here choose I, joy be the consequence.

FIRST FOLIO VERSE NOTES:

In line 12 the word 'stayers' said out loud reveals that it sounds like 'stairs': **See Note 6**.

Remember to pronounce the '-ed' ending, as in 'damned; crisped'; but not the '-'d' endings, like 'deceiv'd; season'd': **See Note 7**.

The separations work well, 'dangerous sea' and 'beautious scarfe', which gives a deliberation to this section: **See Note 20**, as well as the earlier 'as stayers'.

There are 3 mid-line endings: **See Note 18**.

This is a soliloquy at first: **See Note 25**, and he addresses the audience as 'you', but at the climactic moment of choosing he addresses the caskets as 'thou': **See Note 22**.

Editors change 'There is no voice so simple' to 'There is no vice so simple'.

A Midsommer Nights Dreame, II-1

OBERON

I pray thee give it me.
I know a banke where the wilde time blowes,
Where Oxslips and the nodding Violet growes,
Quite over-cannoped with luscious woodbine,
With sweet muske roses, and with Eglantine;
There sleepes *Tytania*, sometime of the night,
Lul'd in these flowers, with dances and delight:
And there the snake throwes her enammel'd skinne,
Weed wide enough to rap a Fairy in.
And with the juyce of this Ile streake her eyes,
And make her full of hatefull fantasies.
Take thou some of it, and seek through this grove;
A sweet *Athenian* Lady is in love
With a disdainefull youth: annoint his eyes,
But doe it when the next thing he espies,
May be the Lady. Thou shalt know the man,
By the *Athenian* garments he hath on.
Effect it with some care, that he may prove
More fond on her, then she upon her love;
And looke thou meet me ere the first Cocke crow.

FIRST FOLIO VERSE NOTES:

After the 1st line, the next 8 lines are all one flowery flowing thought: **See Note 2**; the next 2 lines are straightforward statements.

Line 13 ends with 'is in love' – be careful not to run it on to the next line, but pick it out: **See Note 9**.

There is a mid-line ending towards the end that colours the attitude there: **See Note 18**.

The first half of the speech is full of rich images, and the second half gets down to the factual request: **See Note 22**.

The whole speech is a series of rhyming couplets, except the very last line: **See Note 11**.

The Taming of the Shrew, III-3

PETRUCHIO

Thus have I politickely begun my reigne,
And 'tis my hope to end successefully:
My Faulcon now is sharpe, and passing emptie,
And til she stoope, she must not be full gorg'd,
For then she never lookes upon her lure.
Another way I have to man my Haggard,
To make her come, and know her Keepers call:
That is, to watch her, as we watch these Kites,
That baite, and beate, and will not be obedient:
She eate no meate to day, nor none shall eate.
Last night she slept not, nor to night she shall not:
As with the meate, some undeserved fault
Ile finde about the making of the bed,
And heere Ile fling the pillow, there the boulster,
This way the Coverlet, another way the sheets:
I, and amid this hurlie I intend,
That all is done in reverend care of her,
And in conclusion, she shal watch all night,
And if she chance to nod, Ile raile and brawle,
And with the clamor keepe her stil awake:
This is a way to kil a Wife with kindnesse,
And thus Ile curbe her mad and headstrong humor:
He that knowes better how to tame a shrew,
Now let him speake, 'tis charity to shew.

FIRST FOLIO VERSE NOTES:

This is a humorous soliloquy: **See Note 25**.

The first 5 lines are one thought, not separate ones: **See Note 2**; and the second thought goes all the way down to the word 'eate'. The last 14 lines are also only one thought.

To keep the meter, the '-ed' of such as 'undeserved' and the '-'d' of 'gorg'd' must be acknowledged: **See Note 7**.

There are good uses of alliterations, assonances and repeated words: **See Notes 10 & 13**, and there are 3 consecutive lines starting with the word 'And'.

The final word is pronounced 'show': **See Note 8**.

'Haggard' = wild female inferior hawk.

Troylus and Cressida, Prologue

PROLOGUE

In Troy there lyes the Scene: From Iles of Greece
The Princes Orgillous, their high blood chaf'd
Have to the Port of Athens sent their shippes
Fraught with the ministers and instruments
Of cruell Warre: Sixty and nine that wore
Their Crownets Regall, from th'Athenian bay
Put forth toward Phrygia, and their vow is made
To ransacke Troy, within whose strong emures
The ravish'd *Helen, Menelaus* Queene,
With wanton *Paris* sleepes, and that's the Quarrell.
To *Tenedos* they come,
And the deepe-drawing Barke do there disgorge
Their warlike frautage: now on Dardan Plaines
The fresh and yet unbruised Greekes do pitch
Their brave Pavillions. *Priams* six-gated City,
Dardan and *Timbria, Helias, Chetas, Trojen,*
And *Antenonidus* with massie Staples
And corresponsive and fulfilling Bolts
Stirre up the Sonnes of Troy.
Now Expectation tickling skittish spirits,
On one and other side, Trojan and Greeke,
Sets all on hazard.   And hither am I come,
A Prologue arm'd, but not in confidence
Of Authors pen, or Actors voyce; but suited
In like conditions, as our Argument;
To tell you (faire Beholders) that our Play
Leapes ore the vaunt and firstlings of those broyles,
Beginning in the middle: starting thence away,
To what may be digested in a Play:
Like, or finde fault, do as your pleasures are,
Now good, or bad, 'tis but the chance of Warre.

FIRST FOLIO VERSE NOTES:

This is a soliloquy: **See Note 25**.

The first 10 lines are all one thought leading to 'that's the Quarrell.': **See Note 2**; and this is followed by a half-line: **See Note 17**. The next chunk of thought also ends with a half-line.

There are 2 half lines, with subsequent opportunities for pauses/stage business: **See Note 17**.

A lot of good capitals are to be acknowledged: **See Note 5**.

Keep the meter by defining words like 'chaf'd' and 'unbruised': **See Note 7**.

'Now Expectation tickling skittish spirits,' has both alliteration and assonance: **See Note 10**, leading up to a mid-line ending: **See Note 18**.

The whole speech ends with a rhyming couplet, remembering that 'Warre' very much rhymed with 'are' in Elizabethan days: **See Note 11**.

Some editors change 'Stirre up' to 'Sperr up' (sperr = lock).

Twelfe Night, Or what you will, I-1

ORSINO

If Musicke be the food of Love, play on,
Give me excesse of it: that surfetting,
The appetite may sicken, and so dye.
That straine agen, it had a dying fall:
O, it came ore my eare, like the sweet sound
That breathes upon a banke of Violets;
Stealing, and giving Odour. Enough, no more,
'Tis not so sweet now, as it was before.
O spirit of Love, how quicke and fresh art thou,
That notwithstanding thy capacitie,
Receiveth as the Sea.   Nought enters there,
Of what validity, and pitch so ere,
But falles into abatement, and low price
Even in a minute; so full of shapes is fancie,
That it alone, is high fantasticall.

(*Will you go hunt the Hart?*)

Why so I do, the Noblest that I have:
O when mine eyes did see *Olivia* first,
Me thought she purg'd the ayre of pestilence;
That instant was I turn'd into a Hart,
And my desires like fell and cruell hounds,
Ere since pursue me. How now what newes from her?

FIRST FOLIO VERSE NOTES:

It is essential for the sense of this speech not to end the first line with a full stop: **See Note 2**; it is the beginning of an argument, *not* a statement: **See Note 2**.

There is no pause to allow Orsino to hear and react to 'That straine agen', and the absence of a pause is as much of a note as having one: **See Note 4**, and there are 2 mid-line endings: **See Note 18**.

The assonances of 'O/ore/Odour' might seem to give a certain pomposity to him: **See Note 12**; and the rhyming couplet in the middle of the speech is to be acknowledged: **See Note 11**.

The speech veers between complex and simple and back again, with interesting results: **See Note 21**.

The line is given by Curio – in the original it goes:

> Cu: Will you go hunt my Lord?
>
> Du: What *Curio*?
>
> Cu: The Hart.

Twelfe Night, Or what you will, IV-3
SEBASTIAN

This is the ayre, that is the glorious Sunne,
This pearle she gave me, I do feel't, and see't,
And though tis wonder that enwraps me thus,
Yet 'tis not madnesse.   Where's *Anthonio* then,
I could not finde him at the Elephant,
Yet there he was, and there I found this credite,
That he did range the towne to seeke me out,
His councell now might do me golden service,
For though my soule disputes well with my sence,
That this may be some error, but no madnesse,
Yet doth this accident and flood of Fortune,
So farre exceed all instance, all discourse,
That I am readie to distrust mine eyes,
And wrangle with my reason that perswades me
To any other trust, but that I am mad,
Or else the Ladies mad; yet if 'twere so,
She could not sway her house, command her followers,
Take, and give backe affayres, and their dispatch,
With such a smooth, discreet, and stable bearing
As I perceive she do's: there's something in't
That is deceiveable.   But heere the Lady comes.

FIRST FOLIO VERSE NOTES:

The first line contains a good separation with 'glorious Sunne': **See Note 20**.

The 17 line thought starting after the mid-line ending 'not madnesse', and finishing at the mid-line ending 'That is deceiveable.'. This gives a specific shape to the speech: **See Notes 2 & 18**.

There is a huge contrast between the complexity of the main part of the speech, and the simplicity of the very last sentence: **See Note 21**.

Remember that 'do's' can be pronounced 'does': **See Note 8**.

The Two Gentlemen of Verona, II-3

LAUNCE

Nay, 'twill bee this howre ere I have done
weeping: all the kinde of the *Launces*, have this very
fault: I have receiv'd my proportion, like the prodigious
Sonne, and am going with Sir *Protheus* to the Imperialls
Court: I thinke *Crab* my dog, be the sowrest natured
dogge that lives: My Mother weeping: my Father
wayling: my Sister crying: our Maid howling: our
Catte wringing her hands, and all our house in a great
perplexitie, yet did not this cruell-hearted Curre shedde
one teare: he is a stone, a very pibble stone, and has no
more pitty in him then a dogge: a Jew would have wept
to have seene our parting: why my Grandam having
no eyes, looke you, wept her selfe blinde at my parting:
nay, Ile shew you the manner of it. This shooe is my father: no, this left shooe is my father; no, no, this left
shooe is my mother: nay, that cannot bee so neyther:
yes; it is so, it is so: it hath the worser sole: this shooe
with the hole in it, is my mother: and this my father:
a veng'ance on't, there 'tis: Now sir, this staffe is my sister: for, looke you, she is as white as a lilly, and as
small as a wand: this hat is *Nan* our maid: I am the
dogge: no, the dogge is himselfe, and I am the dogge:
oh, the dogge is me, and I am my selfe: I; so, so: now
come I to my Father; Father, your blessing: now
should not the shooe speake a word for weeping.
now should I kisse my Father; well, hee weepes on:
Now come I to my Mother: Oh that she could speake
now, like a would-woman: well, I kisse her: why
there 'tis; heere's my mothers breath up and downe:
Now come I to my sister; marke the moane she makes:
now the dogge all this while sheds not a teare: nor
speakes a word: but see how I lay the dust with my
teares.

FIRST FOLIO VERSE NOTES:

This is a soliloquy: **See Note 25**.

The whole speech is in prose: **See Note 1**, but the thoughts must still be guided by the punctuation.

All the colons keep the thought rolling on to 'manner of it': for the last 20 lines are all one thought: **See Notes 2 & 3**, and remember that colons can indicate unfinished thoughts.

In theatricalizing it, do not be afraid to illustrate the images: **See Note 24**.

The Tragedie of Anthonie, and Cleopatra, II-2

ENOBARBUS

I will tell you,
The Barge she sat in, like a burnisht Throne
Burnt on the water: the Poope was beaten Gold,
Purple the Sailes: and so perfumed that
The Windes were Love-sicke.
With them the Owers were Silver,
Which to the tune of Flutes kept stroke, and made
The water which they beate, to follow faster;
As amorous of their strokes.   For her owne person,
It beggerd all discription, she did lye
In her Pavillion, cloth of Gold, of Tissue,
O're-picturing that Venus, where we see
The fancie out-worke Nature.   On each side her,
Stood pretty Dimpled Boyes, like smiling Cupids,
With divers coulour'd Fannes whose winde did seeme,
To glove the delicate cheekes which they did coole,
And what they undid did.

Her Gentlewomen, like the Nereides,
So many Mer-maides tended her i'th'eyes,
And made their bends adornings.   At the Helme
A seeming Mer-maide steeres: The Silken Tackle,
Swell with the touches of those Flower-soft hands,
That yarely frame the office.   From the Barge
A strange invisible perfume hits the sense
Of the adjacent Wharfes.   The Citty cast
Her people out upon her: and *Anthony*
Enthron'd i'th'Market-place, did sit alone,
Whisling to'th'ayre: which but for vacancie,
Had gone to gaze on *Cleopater* too,
And made a gap in Nature.

FIRST FOLIO VERSE NOTES:

This is the very first time Enobarbus speaks verse in the play – and interestingly he breaks it with 2 half-lines: **See Note 17**; they are wonderful for an actor, but not so good for all the editors who silently remove them.

The speech is rich in verbal conceits, significant mid-line endings: **See Note 18**; and capitals: **See Note 5**.

To keep the meter, observe the full pronunciation of 'perfumed': **See Note 7**, and the spelling of her name as 'Cleopater' might well be the way he pronounces her name: **See Note 6**.

Editors often change 'glove' to 'glow'.

The gap in the middle is where Agrippa speaks a short line.

The Tragedie of Hamlet, I-2

CLAUDIUS

Though yet of *Hamlet* our deere Brothers death
The memory be greene: and that it us befitted
To beare our hearts in greefe, and our whole Kingdome
To be contracted in one brow of woe:
Yet so farre hath Discretion fought with Nature,
That we with wisest sorrow thinke on him,
Together with remembrance of our selves.
Therefore our sometimes Sister, now our Queen,
Th'Imperiall Joyntresse of this warlike State,
Have we, as 'twere, with a defeated joy,
With one Auspicious, and one Dropping eye,
With mirth in Funerall, and with Dirge in Marriage,
In equall Scale weighing Delight and Dole
Taken to Wife; nor have we heerein barr'd
Your better Wisedomes, which have freely gone
With this affaire along, for all our Thankes.
Now followes, that you know young *Fortinbras*,
Holding a weake supposall of our worth;
Or thinking by our late deere Brothers death,
Our State to be disjoynt, and out of Frame,
Colleagued with the dreame of his Advantage;
He hath not fayl'd to pester us with Message,
Importing the surrender of those Lands
Lost by his Father: with all Bonds of Law
To our most valiant Brother. So much for him.

FIRST FOLIO VERSE NOTES:

The first 3 thoughts of this speech start 'Though'; 'Therefore'; and 'Now followes', giving a specific pattern for the acting of it.

The speech is complex, suddenly ending in 4 simple words: **See Note 21**.

The capitals give a great insight into the speech: **See Note 5**.

The final line's mid-line ending finishes the speech with a bang: **See Note 18**.

In the Folio, Voltemand and Cornelius then enter, and Claudius continues for another 14 lines.

The Tragedie of Hamlet, I-2

HAMLET

Oh that this too too solid Flesh, would melt,
Thaw, and resolve it selfe into a Dew:
Or that the Everlasting had not fixt
His Cannon 'gainst Selfe-slaughter.   O God, O God!
How weary, stale, flat, and unprofitable
Seemes to me all the uses of this world?
Fie on't?   Oh fie, fie, 'tis an unweeded Garden
That growes to Seed: Things rank, and grosse in Nature
Possesse it meerely.   That it should come to this:
But two months dead: Nay, not so much; not two,
So excellent a King, that was to this
Hiperion to a Satyre: so loving to my Mother,
That he might not beteene the windes of heaven
Visit her face too roughly.   Heaven and Earth
Must I remember: why she would hang on him,
As if encrease of Appetite had growne
By what it fed on; and yet within a month?
Let me not thinke on't: Frailty, thy name is woman.
A little Month, or ere those shooes were old,
With which she followed my poore Fathers body
Like *Niobe*, all teares.   Why she, even she.
(O Heaven!   A beast that wants discourse of Reason
Would have mourn'd longer) married with mine Unkle,
My Fathers Brother: but no more like my Father,
Then I to *Hercules*.   Within a Moneth?
Ere yet the salt of most unrighteous Teares
Had left the flushing of her gauled eyes,
She married.   O most wicked speed, to post
With such dexterity to Incestuous sheets:
It is not, nor it cannot come to good.
But breake my heart, for I must hold my tongue.

FIRST FOLIO VERSE NOTES:

This speech is a soliloquy: **See Note 25**.

The first word is 'Oh', not the 'O' which we expect it to be: **See Note 12**.

In the speech, at first the word is 'month', later it is 'Month', and finally 'Moneth' – all different, all to be acted differently: **See Note 6**.

The 8 mid-line endings drive the speech on wonderfully: **See Note 18**.

There is significant assonance on 'O; most; post': **See Note 10**; not forgetting the separations of 'Incestuous sheets': **See Note 20**.

The Tragedie of Hamlet, II-2

HAMLET

I so, God buy'ye: Now I am alone.
Oh what a Rogue and Pesant slave am I?
Is it not monstrous that this Player heere,
But in a Fixion, in a dreame of Passion,
Could force his soule so to his whole conceit,
That from her working, all his visage warm'd;
Teares in his eyes, distraction in's Aspect,
A broken voyce, and his whole Function suiting
With Formes, to his Conceit?   And all for nothing?
For *Hecuba*?
What's *Hecuba* to him, or he to *Hecuba*,
That he should weepe for her?   What would he doe,
Had he the Motive and the Cue for passion
That I have?   He would drowne the Stage with teares,
And cleave the generall eare with horrid speech:
Make mad the guilty, and apale the free,
Confound the ignorant, and amaze indeed,
The very faculty of Eyes and Eares.   Yet I,
A dull and muddy-metled Rascall, peake
Like John a-dreames, unpregnant of my cause,
And can say nothing: No, not for a King,
Upon whose property, and most deere life,
A damn'd defeate was made.   Am I a Coward?
Who calles me Villaine? breakes my pate a-crosse?
Pluckes off my Beard, and blowes it in my face?
Tweakes me by'th'Nose? gives me the Lye i'th'Throate,
As deepe as to the Lungs?   Who does me this?
Ha?   Why I should take it: for it cannot be,
But I am Pigeon-Liver'd, and lacke Gall
To make Oppression bitter, or ere this,
I should have fatted all the Region Kites
With this Slaves Offall, bloudy: a Bawdy villaine,
Remorselesse, Treacherous, Letcherous, kindles villaine!
Oh Vengeance!

FIRST FOLIO VERSE NOTES:

This is a famous soliloquy: **See Note 25**.

It starts with the rolling assonance of 'Oh/Rogue': **See Note 10**, then rushes along for another 7 lines before the end of the thought: **See Note 2**.

There are just 2 words in the line 'For *Hecuba*?', a great opportunity for stage business (pacing about? leaving the stage and returning? tearing hair? etc.): **See Note 17**.

The end word in each line pays a dividend when chosen: **See Note 9**.

Then there are more alliterations and assonances: '*Hecuba*/him/he/*Hecuba*/he/weepe/her' – all giving an indication of the complexity of the mood: **See Note 21**.

The thoughts tend to end mid-line, making this a driving rather than reflective speech: **See Note 18**.

There is a series of question marks that work when played *as* questions, and the speech has been ended in the middle: the final 2 word line is in the middle of the full speech (and so attracts the same clue for pause and/or business).

The final full line is full of the repetition words with the sound 's' in them, so this should be used in the acting: **See Note 23**.

In the Folio the speech goes on for another 23 lines.

The Tragedie of Hamlet, III-1

HAMLET

To be, or not to be, that is the Question:
Whether 'tis Nobler in the minde to suffer
The Slings and Arrowes of outragious Fortune,
Or to take Armes against a Sea of troubles,
And by opposing end them: to dye, to sleepe
No more; and by a sleepe, to say we end
The Heart-ake, and the thousand Naturall shockes
That Flesh is heyre too? 'Tis a consummation
Devoutly to be wish'd. To dye to sleepe,
To sleepe, perchance to Dreame; I, there's the rub,
For in that sleepe of death, what dreames may come,
When we have shuffel'd off this mortall coile,
Must give us pawse. There's the respect
That makes Calamity of so long life:
For who would beare the Whips and Scornes of time,
The Oppressors wrong, the poore mans Contumely,
The pangs of dispriz'd Love, the Lawes delay,
The insolence of Office, and the Spurnes
That patient merit of the unworthy takes,
When he himselfe might his *Quietus* make
With a bare Bodkin? Who would these Fardles beare
To grunt and sweat under a weary life,
But that the dread of something after death,
The undiscovered Countrey, from whose Borne
No Traveller returnes, Puzels the will,
And makes us rather beare those illes we have,
Then flye to others that we know not of.
Thus Conscience does make Cowards of us all,
And thus the Native hew of Resolution
Is sicklied o're, with the pale cast of Thought,
And enterprizes of great pith and moment,
With this regard their Currants turne away,

And loose the name of Action.   Soft you now,
The faire *Ophelia*?   Nimph, in thy Orizons
Be all my sinnes remembred.

FIRST FOLIO VERSE NOTES:

It is, of course, a soliloquy: **See Note 25**.

The speech starts with two most important clues: there is the choice to repeat the phrase 'to be', and there is *no* full stop at the end of the line: **See Notes 2 & 13**; this is the start of a complex argument, not a simple statement of fact.

Where the thoughts end, where the argument is taken forward by the colons and semi-colons is illuminating: **See Note 3**.

The first four thoughts all end mid-line, giving a drive and urgency that is not always reflected in modern performances: **See Note 18**.

The capitalization and alliteration at the end of 'Conscience/ Cowards', together with the repetition of 'thus', focus where the speech has got to: **See Note 10**.

It is interesting and revealing to see that Ophelia is talked to mid-line, a sudden shift of focus, and that she is referred to as 'thy' in contrast to the audience's 'you': **See Note 22**.

'Fardles' = burdens; 'Borne' = boundary; 'Orizons' = prayers.

The Tragedie of Hamlet, III-1

HAMLET

Speake the Speech I pray you, as I pronounc'd
it to you trippingly on the Tongue: But if you mouth it,
as many of your Players do, I had as live the Town-Cryer
had spoke my Lines: Nor do not saw the Ayre too much
your hand thus, but use all gently; for in the verie Torrent, Tempest, and (as I may say) the Whirle-winde of
Passion, you must acquire and beget a Temperance that
may give it Smoothnesse. O it offends mee to the Soule,
to see a robustious Pery-wig-pated Fellow, teare a Passion to tatters, to verie ragges, to split the eares of the
Groundlings: who (for the most part) are capeable of
nothing, but inexplicable dumbe shewes, and noise: I could
have such a Fellow whipt for o're-doing Termagant: it
out-*Herod's Herod*. Pray you avoid it.

Be not too tame neyther: but let your owne
Discretion be your Tutor. Sute the Action to the Word,
the Word to the Action, with this speciall observance:
That you ore-stop not the modestie of Nature; for any
thing so over-done, is from the purpose of Playing, whose
end both at the first and now, was and is, to hold as 'twer
the Mirrour up to Nature; to shew Vertue her owne
Feature, Scorne her owne Image, and the verie Age and
Bodie of the Time, his forme and pressure. Now, this
over-done, or come tardie off, though it make the unskil-
full laugh, cannot but make the Judicious greeve; The
censure of the which One, must in your allowance o're-
way a whole Theater of Others. Oh, there bee Players
that I have seene Play, and heard others praise, and that
highly (not to speake it prophanely) that neyther having
the accent of Christians, nor the gate of Christian, Pagan,

or Norman, have so strutted and bellowed, that I have thought some of Natures Jouerney-men had made men, and not made them well, they imitated Humanity so ab-hominably.

FIRST FOLIO VERSE NOTES:

The speech is in prose: **See Note 1**; the same rules for punctuation apply as for poetry.

The use of capitals is precise – read them out in sequence to get an idea for the whole speech: **See Note 5**.

The thoughts are longer than might be expected – keep the argument going until the full stop is reached: **See Note 2**, especially not end-stopping 'trippingly on the Tongue:'; Mirrour up to Nature;' but letting the colons and semi-colons reveal the argument: **See Note 3**.

There is a nice 'O' to liven things up: **See Note 12**.

The long spelling of 'mee' and 'bee' should be used: **See Note 6**.

The gap is where the Player agrees with Hamlet, and the whole speech an insight as to what Shakespeare felt about actors and acting.

The Tragedie of Hamlet, III-3

CLAUDIUS

Thankes deere my Lord.
Oh my offence is ranke, it smels to heaven,
It hath the primall eldest curse upon't,
A Brothers murther.   Pray can I not,
Though inclination be as sharpe as will:
My stronger guilt, defeats my strong intent,
And like a man to double businesse bound,
I stand in pause where I shall first begin,
And both neglect; what if this cursed hand
Were thicker then it selfe with Brothers blood,
Is there not Raine enough in the sweet Heavens
To wash it white as Snow?   Whereto serves mercy,
But to confront the visage of Offence?
And what's in Prayer, but this two-fold force,
To be fore-stalled ere we come to fall,
Or pardon'd being downe?   Then Ile looke up,
My fault is past.   But oh, what forme of Prayer
Can serve my turne?   Forgive me my foule Murther:
That cannot be, since I am still possest
Of those effects for which I did the Murther.
My Crowne, mine owne Ambition, and my Queene:
May one be pardon'd, and retaine th'offence?
In the corrupted currants of this world,
Offences gilded hand may shove by Justice,
And oft 'tis seene, the wicked prize it selfe
Buyes out the Law; but 'tis not so above,
There is no shuffling, there the Action lyes
In his true Nature, and we our selves compell'd
Even to the teeth and forehead of our faults,
To give in evidence.   What then?   What rests?
Try what Repentance can.   What can it not?
Yet what can it, when one cannot repent?

Oh wretched state!   Oh bosome, blacke as death!
Oh limed soule, that strugling to be free,
Art more ingag'd: Helpe Angels, make assay:
Bow stubborne knees, and heart with strings of Steele,
Be soft as sinewes of the new-borne Babe,
All may be well.

FIRST FOLIO VERSE NOTES:

After the first line, this is a soliloquy: **See Note 25**.

The pun in the second line 'ranke' (meaning both smell and position in society) shows that this is someone struggling to express a complex feeling. The word 'Raine' has also a double meaning: **See Note 15**.

There are 9 mid-line endings that drive the whole speech: **See Notes 18 & 23**.

The order of his list is fascinating: 'Crowne/Ambition/ Queene': **See Note 14**.

All the questions should be acted *as* questions.

The first and last 4 words are very simple compared with the rest of the speech: **See Note 21**.

The Tragedie of Julius Cæsar, I-2

CASSIUS

I know that vertue to be in you *Brutus*,
As well as I do know your outward favour.
Well, Honor is the subject of my Story:
I cannot tell, what you and other men
Thinke of this life: But for my single selfe,
I had as liefe not be, as live to be
In awe of such a Thing, as I my selfe.
I was borne free as *Cæsar*, so were you,
We both have fed as well, and we can both
Endure the Winters cold, as well as hee.
For once, upon a Rawe and Gustie day,
The troubled Tyber, chafing with her Shores,
Cæsar saide to me, Dar'st thou *Cassius* now
Leape in with me into this angry Flood,
And swim to yonder Point? Upon the word,
Accoutred as I was, I plunged in,
And bad him follow: so indeed he did.
The Torrent roar'd, and we did buffet it
With lusty Sinewes, throwing it aside,
And stemming it with hearts of Controversie.
But ere we could arrive the Point propos'd,
Cæsar cride, Helpe me *Cassius*, or I sinke.
I (as *Æneas*, our great Ancestor,
Did from the Flames of Troy, upon his shoulder
The old *Anchyses* beare) so, from the waves of Tyber
Did I the tyred *Cæsar*: And this Man,
Is now become a God, and *Cassius* is
A wretched Creature, and must bend his body,
If *Cæsar* carelesly but nod on him.
He had a Feaver when he was in Spaine,
And when the Fit was on him, I did marke
How he did shake: Tis true, this God did shake,

His Coward lippes did from their colour flye,
And that same Eye, whose bend doth awe the World,
Did loose his Lustre: I did heare him grone:
I, and that Tongue of his, that bad the Romans
Marke him, and write his Speeches in their Bookes,
Alas, it cried, Give me some drinke *Titinius*,
As a sicke Girle: Ye Gods, it doth amaze me,
A man of such a feeble temper should
So get the start of the Majesticke world,
And beare the Palme alone.

FIRST FOLIO VERSE NOTES:

There is a liberal use of capitals in the speech: **See Note 5**.

Cassius addresses the person he is speaking to as 'you', but when reporting Cæsar's words to him, shows that he himself was addressed as 'thou': **See Note 22**.

The speech starts off with some very short thoughts, but the last 13 lines are all one thought: **See Note 2**.

There are assonances all through, especially 'free as *Cæsar*'; 'I the tyred *Cæsar*'; and there are a large number of alliterations too, like 'Point propos'd': **See Note 10**.

He makes a comparison between himself and Æneas; between Cæsar and Anchysses; and finally Man and God.

The Tragedie of Julius Cæsar, I-2

CASSIUS

Why man, he doth bestride the narrow world
Like a Colossus, and we petty men
Walke under his huge legges, and peepe about
To finde our selves dishonourable Graves.
Men at sometime, are Masters of their Fates.
The fault (deere *Brutus*) is not in our Starres,
But in our Selves, that we are underlings.
Brutus and *Cæsar*: What should be in that *Cæsar*?
Why should that name be sounded more then yours
Write them together: Yours, is as faire a Name:
Sound them, it doth become the mouth aswell:
Weigh them, it is as heavy: Conjure with 'em,
Brutus will start a Spirit as soone as *Cæsar*.
Now in the names of all the Gods at once,
Upon what meate doth this our *Cæsar* feede,
That he is growne so great?   Age, thou art sham'd.
Rome, thou hast lost the breed of Noble Bloods.
When went there by an Age, since the great Flood,
But it was fam'd with more then with one man?
When could they say (till now) that talk'd of Rome,
That her wide Walkes incompast but one man?
Now is it Rome indeed, and Roome enough
When there is in it but one onely man.
O! you and I, have heard our Fathers say,
There was a *Brutus* once, that would have brook'd
Th'eternall Divell to keepe his State in Rome,
As easily as a King.

FIRST FOLIO VERSE NOTES:

The strength of the assonances of 'meate/*Cæsar*/feede' gives an attitude of Cassius towards Cæsar: **See Note 10**; followed closely by the alliteration of 'growne/great'.

Cassius addresses Brutus as 'you', but Age and Rome as 'thou': **See Note 22**.

The word man or men is repeated 6 times (and Cæsar 4 times); perhaps the speaker is reminding the listener of Cæsar's lack of divinity.

The single 'O' is more of a noise than the word 'Oh': **See Note 12**.

There are some significant separations: 'doth this'; 'his State': **See Note 20**.

The Tragedie of Julius Cæsar, II-1

BRUTUS

It must be by his death: and for my part,
I know no personall cause, to spurne at him,
But for the generall.   He would be crown'd:
How that might change his nature, there's the question?
It is the bright day, that brings forth the Adder,
And that craves warie walking: Crowne him that,
And then I graunt we put a Sting in him,
That at his will he may doe danger with.
Th'abuse of Greatnesse, is, when it dis-joynes
Remorse from Power: And to speake truth of *Cæsar*,
I have not knowne, when his Affections sway'd
More then his Reason.   But 'tis a common proofe,
That Lowlynesse is young Ambitions Ladder,
Whereto the Climber upward turnes his Face:
But when he once attaines the upmost Round,
He then unto the Ladder turnes his Backe,
Lookes in the Clouds, scorning the base degrees
By which he did ascend: so *Cæsar* may;
Then least he may, prevent.   And since the Quarrell
Will beare no colour, for the thing he is,
Fashion it thus; that what he is, augmented,
Would runne to these, and these extremities:
And therefore thinke him as a Serpents egge,
Which hatch'd, would as his kinde grow mischievous;
And kill him in the shell.

FIRST FOLIO VERSE NOTES:

This is a soliloquy: **See Note 25**.

The first 6 words do not end in a full stop – they are part of an argument, not a statement by itself: **See Note 2**.

A lot of new thoughts start with the unexpected 'And', as if the speaker had had a sudden new idea, and all through the punctuation is unexpected: **See Note 4**.

The capitals are significant here: **See Note 5**.

Good articulation is needed for this speech, with its many separations, such as: 'Affections sway's; But 'tis; Clouds, scorning': **See Note 20**; and there are a lot of sharp little words all close together: **See Note 23**.

There are 3 mid-line endings, which add drive and urgency to the speech: **See Note 18**.

The Tragedie of Julius Cæsar, III-1

MARK ANTONY

O mighty *Cæsar*!   Dost thou lye so lowe?
Are all thy Conquests, Glories, Triumphes, Spoiles,
Shrunke to this little Measure?   Fare thee well.
I know not Gentlemen what you intend,
Who else must be let blood, who else is ranke:
If I my selfe, there is no houre so fit
As *Cæsars* deaths houre;   nor no Instrument
Of halfe that worth, as those your Swords;   made rich
With the most Noble blood of all this World.
I do beseech yee, if you beare me hard,
Now, whil'st your purpled hands do reeke and smoake,
Fulfill your pleasure.   Live a thousand yeeres,
I shall not finde my selfe so apt to dye.
No place will please me so, no meane of death,
As heere by *Cæsar*, and by you cut off,
The Choice and Master Spirits of this Age.

FIRST FOLIO VERSE NOTES:

The speech starts with the sound 'O': **See Note 12**, and ends with two 'O' sounds: **See Note 10**.

In line 2 the list is not one that builds: **See Note 14**.

Mark Anthony addresses Cæsar as 'thou' – and the listeners as 'you': **See Note 22**.

All the capitals give a strong attitude to the piece: **See Note 5**, and the alliteration points out as usual: 'lye/lowe': **See Note 10**.

The long spelling in the penultimate line 'heere' gives a specific slant to this bit of the speech: **See Note 6**.

The Tragedie of Julius Cæsar, III-1

MARK ANTONY

O pardon me, thou bleeding peece of Earth:
That I am meeke and gentle with these Butchers.
Thou art the Ruines of the Noblest man
That ever lived in the Tide of Times.
Woe to the hand that shed this costly Blood.
Over thy wounds, now do I Prophesie,
(Which like dumbe mouthes do ope their Ruby lips,
To begge the voyce and utterance of my Tongue)
A Curse shall light upon the limbes of men;
Domesticke Fury, and fierce Civill strife,
Shall cumber all the parts of Italy:
Blood and destruction shall be so in use,
And dreadfull Objects so familiar,
That Mothers shall but smile, when they behold
Their Infants quartered with the hands of Warre:
All pitty choak'd with custome of fell deeds,
And *Cæsars* Spirit ranging for Revenge,
With *Ate* by his side, come hot from Hell,
Shall in these Confines, with a Monarkes voyce,
Cry havocke, and let slip the Dogges of Warre,
That this foule deede, shall smell above the earth
With Carrion men, groaning for Buriall.

FIRST FOLIO VERSE NOTES:

The speech starts with a wonderful series of assonances that lead it in a surprising direction: 'me/bleeding/peece/meeke/these': **See Note 10**.

There are 3 short thoughts to begin with, and then a long rolling thought that goes on right up to 'groaning for Buriall' — being careful *not* to put a full stop after 'Dogges of Warre': **See Note 2**.

The brackets help in constructing the curse: **See Note 16**.

The separations, such as 'fierce Civill; Objects so; and *Cæsars* Spirit' give a precision to the interpretation: **See Note 20**.

The alliterations add to the pulse of the speech: 'light/limbes; ranging/Revenge; hot/Hell': **See Note 10**.

The Tragedie of Julius Cæsar, III-2

MARK ANTONY

Friends, Romans, Countrymen, lend me your ears:
I come to bury *Cæsar*, not to praise him:
The evill that men do, lives after them,
The good is oft enterred with their bones,
So let it be with *Cæsar*.   The Noble *Brutus*,
Hath told you *Cæsar* was Ambitious:
If it were so, it was a greevous Fault,
And greevously hath *Cæsar* answer'd it.
Heere, under leave of *Brutus*, and the rest
(For *Brutus* is an Honourable man,
So are they all; all Honourable men)
Come I to speake in *Cæsars* Funerall.
He was my Friend, faithfull, and just to me;
But *Brutus* sayes, he was Ambitious,
And *Brutus* is an Honourable man.
He hath brought many Captives home to Rome,
Whose Ransomes, did the generall Coffers fill:
Did this in *Cæsar* seeme Ambitious?
When that the poore have cry'de, *Cæsar* hath wept:
Ambition should be made of sterner stuffe,
Yet *Brutus* sayes, he was Ambitious:
And *Brutus* is an Honourable man.
You all did see, that on the *Lupercall*,
I thrice presented him a Kingly Crowne,
Which he did thrice refuse.   Was this Ambition?
Yet *Brutus* sayes, he was Ambitious:
And sure he is an Honourable man.
I speake not to disproove what *Brutus* spoke,
But heere I am, to speake what I do know;
You all did love him once, not without cause,
What cause with-holds you then, to mourne for him?
O Judgement! thou art fled to brutish Beasts,
And Men have lost their Reason.   Beare with me,

My heart is in the Coffin there with *Cæsar*,
And I must pawse, till it come backe to me.

FIRST FOLIO VERSE NOTES:

Just to go through the speech saying aloud all the words in capitals gives a complete series of stepping stones as to the sense and meaning: **See Note 5**.

There is always a temptation to put in full stops where they do not belong, such as after 'lend me your ears:' and 'not to praise him'; keep the thought packages as long as they are written: **See Note 2**.

The brackets point out the attitude of the speaker: **See Note 16**.

Where there are mid-line endings, and where not, show where the speaker is accelerating, and where sitting back on the delivery: **See Note 18**.

At the end, there is a single 'O', followed by a gear change to 'thou': **See Notes 12 & 22**, and some nice assonances 'Beasts/Reason' that show the speech ends differently to where it started: **See Note 10**.

The Tragedie of King Lear, I-2

BASTARD

Thou Nature art my Goddesse, to thy Law
My services are bound, wherefore should I
Stand in the plague of custome, and permit
The curiosity of Nations, to deprive me?
For that I am some twelve, or fourteene Moonshines
Lag of a Brother?   Why Bastard?   Wherefore base?
When my Dimensions are as well compact,
My minde as generous, and my shape as true
As honest Madams issue?   Why brand they us
With Base?   With basenes Barstadie?   Base, Base?
Who in the lustie stealth of Nature, take
More composition, and fierce qualitie,
Then doth within a dull stale tyred bed
Goe to th'creating a whole tribe of Fops
Got 'tweene a sleepe, and wake?   Well then,
Legitimate *Edgar*, I must have your land,
Our Fathers love, is to the Bastard *Edmond*,
As to th'legitimate: fine word: Legitimate.
Well, my Legittimate, if this Letter speed,
And my invention thrive, *Edmond* the base
Shall to'th'Legitimate: I grow, I prosper:
Now Gods, stand up for Bastards.

FIRST FOLIO VERSE NOTES:

This is a soliloquy: **See Note 25**.

The end words of each line need to be chosen carefully: **See Note 9**; and the end of the line 'deprive me?' seems odd — and that is the acting note: **See Note 4**.

There is a precise and accurate use of capitals: **See Note 5**.

All the images of 'grow; prosper; stand' can also apply to the most intimate masculine parts — and this ties in well with the sense of the speech: **See Note 15**.

The mid-line endings stop it being reflective: **See Note 18**, as well as the liberal use of question marks.

The many uses of the words 'Bastard' and 'Base' cry out to be used: **See Note 13**.

Editors change 'Shall to'th'Legitimate' to 'Shall top th'Legitimate'.

The Tragedie of King Lear, II-2

EDGAR

I heard my selfe proclaim'd,
And by the happy hollow of a Tree,
Escap'd the hunt.   No Port is free, no place
That guard, and most unusall vigilance
Do's not attend my taking.   Whiles I may scape
I will preserve myselfe: and am bethought
To take the basest, and most poorest shape
That ever penury in contempt of man,
Brought neere to beast; my face Ile grime with filth,
Blanket my loines, elfe all my haires in knots,
And with presented nakednesse out-face
The Windes, and persecutions of the skie;
The Country gives me proofe, and president
Of Bedlam beggers, who with roaring voices,
Strike in their num'd and mortified Armes,
Pins, Wodden-prickes, Nayles, Sprigs of Rosemarie:
And with this horrible object, from low Farmes,
Poore pelting Villages, Sheeps-Coates, and Milles,
Sometimes with Lunaticke bans, sometime with Praiers
Inforce their charitie: poore *Turlygod* poore *Tom*,
That's something yet: *Edgar* I nothing am.

FIRST FOLIO VERSE NOTES:

This is a soliloquy: **See Note 25**.

The last 17 lines are all one thought: **See Note 2**, preceded by 2 mid-line endings: **See Note 18**; a pattern for the whole can therefore be seen.

There are some very significant capitalized words: **See Note 5**.

The lists are useful: **See Note 14**.

'pelting' = paltry.

The Tragedie of Macbeth, I-2

CAPTAINE

Doubtfull it stood,
As two spent Swimmers, that doe cling together,
And choake their Art: The mercilesse *Macdonwald*
(Worthie to be a Rebell, for to that
The multiplying Villanies of Nature
Doe swarme upon him) from the Westerne Isles
Of Kernes and Gallowgrosses is supply'd,
And Fortune on his damned Quarry smiling,
Shew'd like a Rebells Whore: but all's too weake:
For brave *Macbeth* (well hee deserves that Name)
Disdayning Fortune, with his brandisht Steele,
Which smoak'd with bloody execution
(Like Valours Minion) carv'd out his passage,
Till hee fac'd the Slave:
Which nev'r shooke hands, nor bad farwell to him,
Till he unseam'd him from the Nave to th'Chops,
And fix'd his Head upon our Battlements.

As whence the Sunne 'gins his reflection,
Shipwracking Stormes, and direfull Thunders:
So from that Spring, whence comfort seem'd to come,
Discomfort swells: Marke King of Scotland, marke,
No sooner Justice had, with Valour arm'd,
Compell'd these skipping Kernes to trust their heeles,
But the Norweyan Lord, surveying vantage,
With furbusht Armes, and new supplyes of men,
Began a fresh assault.

FIRST FOLIO VERSE NOTES:

There are 3 lots of brackets here: **See Note 16**.

The long spelling of 'hee' adds to the interpretation: **See Note 6**.

In the middle of the speech is a half-line (is the Captaine fainting? overwhelmed in the presence of his king?): **See Note 17**. Other lines, like 'Shipwracking Stormes ...', are incomplete.

There is a good separation for 'Marke King of Scotland': **See Note 20**.

The gap in the speech is where Duncan has a brief interpolation.

Editors change 'Gallowgrosses' to 'gallowglasses'; and 'Quarry' to 'quarrel'.

The Tragedie of Macbeth, I-7

MACBETH

If it were done, when 'tis done, then 'twer well,
It were done quickly: If th'Assassination
Could trammell up the Consequence, and catch
With his surcease, Successe: that but this blow
Might be the be all, and the end all.   Heere,
But heere, upon this Banke and Schoole of time,
Wee'ld jumpe the life to come.   But in these Cases,
We still have judgement heere, that we but teach
Bloody Instructions, which being taught, returne
To plague th'Inventer, This even-handed Justice
Commends th'Ingredience of our poyson'd Challice
To our owne lips.   Hee's heere in double trust;
First, as I am his Kinsman, and his Subject,
Strong both against the Deed: Then, as his Host,
Who should against his Murtherer shut the doore,
Not beare the knife my selfe.   Besides, this *Duncane*
Hath borne his Faculties so meeke; hath bin
So cleere in his great Office, that his Vertues
Will pleade like Angels, Trumpet-tongu'd against
The deepe damnation of his taking off:
And Pitty, like a naked New-borne-Babe,
Striding the blast, or Heavens Cherubin, hors'd
Upon the sightlesse Curriors of the Ayre,
Shall blow the horrid deed in every eye,
That teares shall drowne the winde.   I have no Spurre
To pricke the sides of my intent, but onely
Vaulting Ambition, which ore-leapes it selfe,
And falles on th'other.

FIRST FOLIO VERSE NOTES:

This is a soliloquy for Macbeth: **See Note 25**.

The word 'done' is repeated 3 times in the first 2 lines: **See Note 13**.

There is no full stop after 'quickly' in the second line, which changes the meaning and interpretation: **See Note 3**.

Notice the large number of mid-line endings: **See Note 18**.

In line 6 the word 'Banke' means a school bench, which matches the word 'Schoole', and later 'teach' and 'taught'. Editors often mistakenly change the word to 'shoal'.

The capitals are significant: **See Note 5**, as well as the elongated spelling of 'heere': **See Note 6**.

The Tragedie of Macbeth, II-1

MACBETH

Goe bid thy Mistresse, when my drinke is ready,
She strike upon the Bell.   Get thee to bed.

EXIT SERVANT.

Is this a Dagger, which I see before me,
The Handle toward my Hand?   Come, let me clutch thee:
I have thee not, and yet I see thee still.
Art thou not fatall Vision, sensible
To feeling, as to sight? or art thou but
A Dagger of the Minde, a false Creation,
Proceeding from the heat-oppressed Braine?
I see thee yet, in forme as palpable,
As this which now I draw.
Thou marshall'st me the way that I was going,
And such an Instrument I was to use.
Mine Eyes are made the fooles o'th'other Sences,
Or else worth all the rest: I see thee still;
And on thy Blade, and Dudgeon, Gouts of Blood,
Which was not so before.   There's no such thing:
It is the bloody Businesse, which informes
Thus to mine Eyes.   Now o're the one halfe World
Nature seemes dead, and wicked Dreames abuse
The Curtain'd sleepe: Witchcraft celebrates
Pale *Heccats* Offrings: and wither'd Murther,
Alarum'd by his Centinell, the Wolfe,
Whose howle's his Watch, thus with his stealthy pace,
With *Tarquins* ravishing sides, towards his designe
Moves like a Ghost.   Thou sowre and firme-set Earth
Heare not my steps, which they may walke, for feare
Thy very stones prate of my where-about,
And take the present horror from the time,

Which now sutes with it.   Whiles I threat, he lives:
Words to the heat of deedes too cold breath gives.

A BELL RINGS.

I goe, and it is done: the Bell invites me.
Heare it not, *Duncan*, for it is a Knell,
That summons thee to Heaven, or to Hell.

FIRST FOLIO VERSE NOTES:

This is a soliloquy: **See Note 25**.

There is a half-line for business (presumably to do with drawing a dagger): **See Note 17**.

The 5th line 'The Handle ...' is an Alexandrine: **See Note 9**.

There are mid-line endings that add to the drive of the speech: **See Note 18**, as well as give Macbeth some mercurial thought changes.

The end words need to be chosen carefully and not run on (enjambed): **See Note 9**.

Editors change '*Tarquins* ravishing sides' to '*Tarquins* ravishing strides'; 'Thou sowre and firme-set Earth' to 'Thou sure and firme-set Earth'; and 'which they may walke' to 'which way they walke'.

'Gouts' = drops.

The Tragedie of Macbeth, II-3

PORTER

KNOCKING WITHIN.

Here's a knocking indeede: if a man were
Porter of Hell Gate, hee should have old turning the
Key.   *KNOCK.*   Knock, Knock, Knock. Who's there
i'th'name of *Belzebub*?   Here's a Farmer, that hang'd
himselfe on th'expectation of Plentie: Come in time, have
Napkins enow about you, here you'le sweat for't.   *KNOCK.*
Knock, knock.   Who's there in th'other Devils Name?
Faith here's an Equivocator, that could sweare in both
the Scales against eyther Scale, who committed Treason
enough for Gods sake, yet could not equivocate to Hea-
ven: oh come in, Equivocator.   *KNOCK.*   Knock,
Knock, Knock.   Who's there?   'Faith here's an English
Taylor come hither, for stealing out of a French Hose:
Come in Taylor, here you may rost your Goose.   *KNOCK.*
Knock, Knock.   Never at quiet: What are you? but this
place is too cold for Hell.   Ile Devill-Porter it no further:
I had thought to have let in some of all Professions, that
goe the Primrose way to th'everlasting Bonfire.   *KNOCK.*
Anon, anon, I pray you remember the Porter.

FIRST FOLIO VERSE NOTES:

The whole speech is a soliloquy, and is in prose: **See Notes 1 & 25**, so it is more personality acting, even though the rules for capitalization and punctuation still hold.

The long spelling of 'hee' at the start points out the attitude: **See Note 6**.

There needs to be an acting reason why the door is not opened at once — a reason for the Porter to deliver the speech.

The last line can as easily be given to the audience (remember who it was that made you laugh) as it is to the incoming Macduff and Lenox.

The joke about French Hose is that it was incredibly skimpy.

'rost your Goose' = heat your iron.

The Tragedie of Macbeth, III-1

MACBETH

Bring them before us.

EXIT SERVANT.

To be thus, is nothing, but to be safely thus:
Our feares in *Banquo* sticke deepe,
And in his Royaltie of Nature reignes that
Which would be fear'd.   'Tis much he dares,
And to that dauntlesse temper of his Minde,
He hath a Wisdome, that doth guide his Valour,
To act in safetie.   There is none but he,
Whose being I doe feare: and under him,
My *Genius* is rebuk'd, as it is said
Mark Anthonies was by *Cæsar.*   He chid the Sisters,
When first they put the Name of King upon me,
And bad them speake to him.   Then Prophet-like,
They hayl'd him Father to a Line of Kings.
Upon my Head they plac'd a fruitlesse Crowne,
And put a barren Scepter in my Gripe,
Thence to be wrencht with an unlineall Hand,
No Sonne of mine succeeding: if't be so,
For *Banquo's* Issue have I fil'd my Minde,
For them, the gracious *Duncan* have I murther'd,
Put Rancours in the Vessell of my Peace
Onely for them, and mine eternall Jewell
Given to the common Enemie of Man,
To make them Kings, the Seedes of *Banquo* Kings.
Rather then so, come Fate into the Lyst,
And champion me to th'utterance.
Who's there?

FIRST FOLIO VERSE NOTES:

All except the last line is a soliloquy: **See Note 25**.

The thoughts (except one near the end 'the Seedes of *Banquo* Kings.') all end with a mid-line ending: **See Note 18**, a big clue as to how to give the speech: **See Note 23**.

The second line, and the one starting '*Mark Anthonies* was by *Cæsar* ...', are both Alexandrines: **See Note 9**.

The 3rd line: 'Our feares ...' and the one starting 'Which would be fear'd ...' are not full lines: **See Note 17**.

The capitals give a good insight into the speech: **See Note 5**.

There is a lovely group of assonances: 'I fil'd my Minde': **See Note 10**.

The Tragedie of Othello, II-1

IAGO

That *Cassio* loves her, I do well beleev't:
That she loves him, 'tis apt, and of great Credite.
The Moore (howbeit that I endure him not)
Is of a constant, loving, Noble Nature,
And I dare thinke, he'le prove to *Desdemona*
A most deere husband.   Now I do love her too,
Not out of absolute Lust, (though peradventure
I stand accomptant for as great a sin)
But partely led to dyet my Revenge,
For that I do suspect the lustie Moore
Hath leap'd into my Seate.   The thought whereof,
Doth (like a poysonous Minerall) gnaw my Inwardes:
And nothing can, or shall content my Soule
Till I am eeven'd with him, wife, for wife.
Or fayling so, yet that I put the Moore,
At least into a Jelouzie so strong
That judgement cannot cure.   Which thing to do,
If this poore Trash of Venice, whom I trace
For his quicke hunting, stand the putting on,
Ile have our *Michael Cassio* on the hip,
Abuse him to the Moore, in the right garbe
(For I feare *Cassio* with my Night-Cape too)
Make the Moore thanke me, love me, and reward me,
For making him egregiously an Asse,
And practising upon his peace, and quiet,
Even to madnesse.   'Tis heere: but yet confus'd,
Knaveries plaine face, is never seene, till us'd.

FIRST FOLIO VERSE NOTES:

This is a soliloquy for Iago: **See Note 25**; remembering that characters in soliloquies do not always tell the truth, the line 'For I feare *Cassio* with my Night-Cape too' may only be what Iago wants the audience to believe, not necessarily what he believes.

The use of the word 'Cape' is more encompassing than the puny 'Cap' that editors want to change it to.

In the 3rd line the assonance between 'Moore' and 'endure' gives an extra point to the idea: **See Note 10**.

The mid-line endings are not always predictable: **See Note 18**.

The line ending 'wife, for wife.' *does* end with a full stop: (See Note 4), leading the next thought to start with 'Or fayling so,'.

There are a lot of brackets used: **See Notes 16 & 23**.

Editors change 'in the right garbe' to 'in the rank garbe'.

The Tragedie of Othello, II-3

IAGO

And what's he then,
That saies I play the Villaine?
When this advise is free I give, and honest,
Proball to thinking, and indeed the course
To win the Moore againe.
For 'tis most easie
Th'inclyning *Desdemona* to subdue
In any honest Suite.   She's fram'd as fruitefull
As the free Elements.   And then for her
To win the Moore, were to renownce his Baptisme,
All Seales, and Simbols of redeemed sin:
His Soule is so enfetter'd to her Love,
That she may make, unmake, do what she list,
Even as her Appetite shall play the God,
With his weake Function.   How am I then a Villaine,
To Counsell *Cassio* to this paralell course,
Directly to his good? Divinitie of hell,
When divels will the blackest sinnes put on,
They do suggest at first with heavenly shewes,
As I do now.   For whiles this honest Foole
Plies *Desdemona*, to repaire his Fortune,
And she for him, pleades strongly to the Moore,
Ile powre this pestilence into his eare:
That she repeales him, for her bodies Lust,
And by how much she strives to do him good,
She shall undo her Credite with the Moore.
So will I turne her vertue into pitch,
And out of her owne goodnesse make the Net,
That shall en-mash them all.
How now *Rodorigo*?

FIRST FOLIO VERSE NOTES:

This is a soliloquy: **See Note 25**, that starting with a half line might indicate coming in on cue with the speech, but the next line also being incomplete shows that there are pauses around: **See Note 17**.

There are another 3 half-lines, with corresponding acting consequences.

There is a lot of alliteration around the letter 's', that can give a hissing quality to the whole: **See Note 10**, and a lovely assonance between 'Moore' and 'powre'.

The mid-line endings again show the drive of the speech: **See Note 18**.

The Tragedie of Othello, V-2

OTHELLO

It is the Cause, it is the Cause (my Soule)
Let me not name it to you, you chaste Starres,
It is the Cause.   Yet Ile not shed her blood,
Nor scarre that whiter skin of hers, then Snow,
And smooth as Monumentall Alablaster:
Yet she must dye, else shee'l betray more men:
Put out the Light, and then put out the Light:
If I quench thee, thou flaming Minister,
I can againe thy former light restore,
Should I repent me.   But once put out thy Light,
Thou cunning'st Patterne of excelling Nature,
I know not where is that *Promethæan* heate
That can thy Light re-Lume.
When I have pluck'd thy Rose,
I cannot give it vitall growth againe,
It needs must wither.   Ile smell thee on the Tree.
Oh Balmy breath, that dost almost perswade
Justice to breake her Sword.   One more, one more:
Be thus when thou art dead, and I will kill thee,
And love thee after.   One more, and that's the last.
So sweet, was ne're so fatall.   I must weepe,
But they are cruell Teares: This sorrow's heavenly,
It strikes, where it doth love.   She wakes.

FIRST FOLIO VERSE NOTES:

This is a soliloquy as Othello stands over the sleeping Desdemona: **See Note 25**.

The repetition of the word 'Cause' is immediately followed by a mid-line ending: **See Notes 13 & 18**.

He changes from calling the starres 'you' to calling Desdemona 'thee': **See Note 22**, giving an insight into his mood.

There are 2 half-lines where he makes a decision: **See Note 17**.

The colons point to the force of the argument: **See Note 3**, make sure it is not simply a series of statements.

The capitals are interesting as to which word is capitalized and which not: **See Note 5**.

The Tragedie of Romeo and Juliet, II-1

ROMEO

He jeasts at Scarres that never felt a wound,
But soft, what light through yonder window breaks?
It is the East, and *Juliet* is the Sunne,
Arise faire Sun and kill the envious Moone,
Who is already sicke and pale with griefe,
That thou her Maid art far more faire then she:
Be not her Maid since she is envious,
Her Vestal livery is but sicke and greene,
And none but fooles do weare it, cast it off:
It is my Lady, O it is my Love, O that she knew she were,
She speakes, yet she sayes nothing, what of that?
Her eye discourses, I will answere it:
I am too bold 'tis not to me she speakes:
Two of the fairest starres in all the Heaven,
Having some businesse do entreat her eyes,
To twinckle in their Spheres till they returne.
What if her eyes were there, they in her head,
The brightnesse of her cheeke would shame those starres,
As day-light doth a Lampe, her eye in heaven,
Would through the ayrie Region streame so bright,
That Birds would sing, and thinke it were not night:
See how she leanes her cheeke upon her hand.
O that I were a Glove upon that hand,
That I might touch that cheeke.

FIRST FOLIO VERSE NOTES:

The speech starts with a very long thought that goes on and on: **See Note 2**.

The line 'It is my Lady, ...' is a very long one: **See Note 17**.

In the speech 3 times the word is a single O: **See Note 12**.

There is a good separation 'those starres': **See Note 5**, which brings out the repeated image.

The assonance 'leanes her cheeke' adds to his attitude and mood: **See Note 10**.

There are a lot of complex images in the speech — but the last line is very simple indeed: **See Note 21**.

The Tragedie of Romeo and Juliet, II-3

FRIER LAWRENCE

The gray ey'd morne smiles on the frowning night,
Checkring the Easterne Cloudes with streaks of light:
And fleckled darknesse like a drunkard reeles,
From forth daies path, and *Titans* burning wheeles:
Now ere the Sun advance his burning eye,
The day to cheere, and nights danke dew to dry,
I must upfill this Osier Cage of ours,
With balefull weedes, and precious Juiced flowers,
The earth that's Natures mother, is her Tombe,
What is her burying grave that is her wombe:
And from her wombe children of divers kind
We sucking on her naturall bosome find:
Many for many vertues excellent:
None but for some, and yet all different.
O mickle is the powerfull grace that lies
In Plants, Hearbs, stones, and their true qualities:
For nought so vile, that on the earth doth live,
But to the earth some speciall good doth give.
Nor ought so good, but strain'd from that faire use,
Revolts from true birth, stumbling on abuse.
Vertue it selfe turnes vice being misapplied,
And vice sometime by action dignified.

ENTER ROMEO.

Within the infant rin'd of this weake flower,
Poyson hath residence, and medicine power:
For this being smelt, with that part cheares each part,
Being tasted slayes all sences with the heart.

Two such opposed Kings encampe them still,
In man as well as Hearbes, grace and rude will:
And where the worser is predominant,
Full soone the Canker death eates up that Plant.

FIRST FOLIO VERSE NOTES:

This is a soliloquy: **See Note 25**.

It is all one long thought up to 'and yet all different': **See Note 2**.

All through the punctuation is important to acknowledge, particularly the argument arising out of using the colons: **See Note 3**.

The sense is changed if, for instance, a full stop is incorrectly put after 'medicine power', changing an argument into a statement: **See Note 4**.

Romeo enters in the middle, and therefore hears the rest of the speech.

The last part of the speech is more factual, with a moral at the end: **See Note 21**.

'Osier Cage' = willow basket; 'mickle' = great.

The Tragedie of Romeo and Juliet, III-1

BENVOLIO

Tybalt here slaine, whom *Romeo's* hand did slay,
Romeo that spoke him faire, bid him bethinke
How nice the Quarrell was, and urg'd withall
Your high displeasure: all this uttered,
With gentle breath, calme looke, knees humbly bow'd
Could not take truce with the unruly spleene
Of *Tybalts* deafe to peace, but that he Tilts
With Peircing steele at bold *Mercutio's* breast,
Who all as hot, turnes deadly point to point,
And with a Martiall scorne, with one hand beates
Cold death aside, and with the other sends
It back to *Tybalt*, whose dexterity
Retorts it: *Romeo* he cries aloud,
Hold Friends, Friends part, and swifter then his tongue,
His aged arme, beats downe their fatall points,
And twixt them rushes, underneath whose arme,
An envious thrust from *Tybalt*, hit the life
Of stout *Mercutio*, and then *Tybalt* fled.
But by and by comes backe to *Romeo*,
Who had but newly entertained Revenge,
And too't they goe like lightning, for ere I
Could draw to part them, was stout *Tybalt* slaine:
And as he fell, did *Romeo* turne and flie:
This is the truth, or let *Benvolio* die.

FIRST FOLIO VERSE NOTES:

In the original presentation of the play, the actors playing Mercutio and Romeo would not have had access to this speech by Benvolio — and so would not necessarily have behaved according to this description. A bold thought — descriptive passages may well be the invention of the speaker: **See Note 4**.

The first thought goes on for a while: **See Note 2**.

To keep the meter, the '-ed' endings such as 'uttered; aged' need to be used: **See Note 7**.

The last word in the line 'for ere I' shows Benvolio emphasising his careful role in the disorder: **See Note 9**.

The speech ends with a rhyming couplet: **See Note 11**.

Editors change 'His aged arme' to 'His agile arme'.

The Lamentable Tragedy
of Titus Andronicus, II-1

AARON

For shame be friends, and joyne for that you jar:
'Tis pollicie, and stratageme must doe
That you affect, and so must you resolve,
That what you cannot as you would atcheive,
You must perforce accomplish as you may:
Take this of me, *Lucrece* was not more chast
Then this *Lavinia*, *Bassianus* love,
A speedier course this lingring languishment
Must we pursue, and I have found the path:
My Lords, a solemne hunting is in hand.
There will the lovely Roman Ladies troope:
The Forrest walkes are wide and spacious,
And many unfrequented plots there are,
Fitted by kinde for rape and villanie:
Single you thither then this dainty Doe,
And strike her home by force, if not by words:
This way or not at all, stand you in hope.
Come, come, our Empresse with her sacred wit
To villainie and vengance consecrate,
Will we acquaint with all that we intend,
And she shall file our engines with advise,
That will not suffer you to square your selves,
But to your wishes height advance you both.
The Emperours Court is like the house of Fame,
The pallace full of tongues, of eyes, of eares:
The Woods are ruthlesse, dreadfull, deafe, and dull:
There speake, and strike brave Boyes, and take your turnes.
There serve your lusts, shadow'd from heavens eye,
And revell in *Lavinia's* Treasurie.

FIRST FOLIO VERSE NOTES:

It is 10 lines until there is a full stop: **See Note 2**, and the subsequent thoughts are long as well.

There is a double entendre on the word 'stand': **See Note 15**.

The alliterations of 'joyne/jar', 'dainty Doe' and 'dreadfull/deafe/dull:' give a direction for the mood of the piece: **See Note 10**.

The particular words in capitals are significant: **See Note 5**.

Editors change 'this lingring languishment' to 'than lingring languishment'.

The Tragedie of Cymbeline, II-2

IACHIMO

IACHIMO FROM THE TRUNKE.

The Crickets sing, and mans ore-labor'd sense
Repaires it selfe by rest: Our *Tarquine* thus
Did softly presse the Rushes, ere he waken'd
The Chastitie he wounded. *Cytherea*,
How bravely thou becom'st thy Bed; fresh Lilly,
And whiter then the Sheetes: that I might touch,
But kisse, one kisse. Rubies unparagon'd,
How deerely they doo't: 'Tis her breathing that
Perfumes the Chamber thus: the Flame o'th'Taper
Bowes toward her, and would under-peepe her lids.
To see th'inclosed Lights, now Canopied
Under these windowes, White and Azure lac'd
With Blew of Heavens owne tinct. But my designe.
To note the Chamber, I will write all downe,
Such, and such pictures: There the window, such
Th'adornement of her Bed; the Arras, Figures,
Why such, and such: and the Contents o'th'Story.
Ah, but some naturall notes about her Body,
Above ten thousand meaner Moveables
Would testifie, t'enrich mine Inventorie.
O sleepe, thou Ape of death, lye dull upon her,
And be her Sense but as a Monument,
Thus in a Chappell lying. Come off, come off;
As slippery as the Gordian-knot was hard.
'Tis mine, and this will witnesse outwardly,
As strongly as the Conscience do's within:
To'th'madding of her Lord. On her left brest
A mole Cinque-spotted: Like the Crimson drops
I'th'bottome of a Cowslippe. Heere's a Voucher,
Stronger then ever Law could make; this Secret
Will force him thinke I have pick'd the lock, and t'ane

The treasure of her Honour.   No more: to what end?
Why should I write this downe, that's riveted,
Screw'd to my memorie.   She hath bin reading late,
The Tale of *Tereus*, heere the leaffe's turn'd downe
Where *Philomele* gave up.   I have enough,
To'th'Truncke againe, and shut the spring of it.
Swift, swift, you Dragons of the night, that dawning
May beare the Ravens eye: I lodge in feare,
Though this a heavenly Angell: hell is heere.

CLOCKE STRIKES.

One, two, three: time, time.

FIRST FOLIO VERSE NOTES:

This is a soliloquy that allows the performer either to walk around the chamber describing it, or to inform the audience directly what they could be seeing: **See Note 25**.

There is a separation in the first line: 'Crickets sing': **See Note 20**, and there are many involving the letter 's': 'As slippery; As strongly; this Secret' all using the hissing sound: **See Note 23**.

The mid-line endings show it is a speech driven on, not full of pauses for business: **See Note 18**, and one thought is just 3 words: 'But my design.'

The word 'such' is repeated 5 times: **See Note 13**.

The speech is littered with capitals: **See Note 5**, and the pun on 'I' and 'eye' shows it to be a speech rich with verbal conceits.

'Cytherea' = Venus.

The Tragedie of Cymbeline, II-5

POSTHUMUS

Is there no way for Men to be, but Women
Must be halfe-workers?   We are all Bastards,
And that most venerable man, which I
Did call my Father, was, I know not where
When I was stampt.   Some Coyner with his Tooles
Made me a counterfeit: yet my Mother seem'd
The *Dian* of that time: so doth my Wife
The Non-pareill of this.   Oh Vengeance, Vengeance!
Me of my lawfull pleasure she restrain'd,
And pray'd me oft forbearance: did it with
A pudencie so Rosie, the sweet view on't
Might well have warm'd olde Saturne;
That I thought her
As Chaste, as un-Sunn'd Snow.   Oh, all the Divels!
This yellow *Iachimo* in an houre, was't not?
Or lesse; at first?   Perchance he spoke not, but
Like a full Acorn'd Boare, a Jarmen on,
Cry'de oh, and mounted; found no opposition
But what he look'd for, should oppose, and she
Should from encounter guard.   Could I finde out
The Womans part in me, for there's no motion
That tends to vice in man, but I affirme
It is the Womans part: be it Lying, note it,
The womans: Flattering, hers; Deceiving, hers:
Lust, and ranke thoughts, hers, hers: Revenges hers:
Ambitions, Covetings, change of Prides, Disdaine,
Nice-longing, Slanders, Mutability;
All Faults that name, nay, that Hell knowes,
Why hers, in part, or all: but rather all For even to Vice
They are not constant, but are changing still;
One Vice, but of a minute old, for one
Not halfe so old as that.   Ile write against them,
Detest them, curse them: yet 'tis greater Skill

In a true Hate, to pray they have their will:
The very Divels cannot plague them better.

FIRST FOLIO VERSE NOTES:

This is a soliloquy: **See Note 25**.

It has many non regular lines and half lines: **See Note 17**, and so it might be seen to stop and start.

The whole speech is also full of mid-line endings: **See Note 18**.

There is a pun in the first line between 'Men' and 'Women' (or Woe Men), and the word 'Jarmen' could be an indication of its pronunciation: **See Note 6**.

The word 'hers' is repeated: **See Note 13**.

There are some good alliterations, such as 'yellow *Iachimo*': **See Note 10**.

The assonances at the end 'Ile write' brings out the feebleness of Posthumus' idea of revenge — not slay or kill as we might expect, but 'write': **See Note 4**.

Editors change 'a Jarmen on' to 'a German one'. They also put 'For even to Vice' on a separate line.

'pudencie' = modesty.

The Tempest, Epilogue

PROSPERO

Now my Charmes are all ore-throwne,
And what strength I have's mine owne.
Which is most faint: now 'tis true
I must be heere confinde by you,
Or sent to *Naples*, Let me not
Since I have my Dukedome got,
And pardon'd the deceiver, dwell
In this bare Island, by your Spell,
But release me from my bands
With the helpe of your good hands:
Gentle breath of yours, my Sailes
Must fill, or else my project failes,
Which was to please: Now I want
Spirits to enforce: Art to inchant,
And my ending is despaire,
Unlesse I be reliev'd by praier
Which pierces so, that it assaults
Mercy it selfe, and frees all faults.
　　As you from crimes would pardon'd be,
　　Let your Indulgence set me free.

FIRST FOLIO VERSE NOTES:

This is a soliloquy: **See Note 25**.

The whole speech is not in iambic pentameters: **See Note 19**.

The middle thought is 16 lines long: **See Note 2**, and the colons define the argument: **See Note 3**.

There are rhyming couplets throughout: **See Note 11**.

The Life of Tymon of Athens, IV-1

TIMON

Let me looke backe upon thee.   O thou Wall
That girdles in those Wolves, dive in the earth,
And fence not Athens.   Matrons, turne incontinent,
Obedience fayle in Children: Slaves and Fooles
Plucke the grave wrinkled Senate from the Bench,
And minister in their steeds, to generall Filthes.
Convert o'th'Instant greene Virginity,
Doo't in your Parents eyes.   Bankrupts, hold fast
Rather then render backe; out with your Knives,
And cut your Trusters throates.   Bound Servants, steale,
Large-handed Robbers your grave Masters are,
And pill by Law.   Maide, to thy Masters bed,
Thy Mistris is o'th'Brothell.   Some of sixteen,
Plucke the lyn'd Crutch from thy old limping Sire,
With it, beate out his Braines.   Piety, and Feare,
Religion to the Gods, Peace, Justice, Truth,
Domesticke awe, Night-rest, and Neighbour-hood,
Instruction, Manners, Mysteries, and Trades,
Degrees, Observances, Customes, and Lawes,
Decline to your confounding contraries.
And yet Confusion live: Plagues incident to men,
Your potent and infectious Feavors, heape
On Athens ripe for stroke.   Thou cold Sciatica,
Cripple our Senators, that their limbes may halt
As lamely as their Manners.   Lust, and Libertie
Creepe in the Mindes and Marrowes of our youth,
That 'gainst the streame of Vertue they may strive,
And drowne themselves in Riot.   Itches, Blaines,
Sowe all th'Athenian bosomes, and their crop
Be generall Leprosie: Breath, infect breath,

That their Society (as their Friendship) may
Be meerely poyson.   Nothing Ile beare from thee
But nakednesse, thou detestable Towne,
Take thou that too, with multiplying Bannes:
Timon will to the Woods, where he shall finde
Th'unkindest Beast, more kinder then Mankinde.
The Gods confound (heare me you good Gods all)
Th'Athenians both within and out that Wall:
And graunt as *Timon* growes, his hate may grow
To the whole race of Mankinde, high and low.
Amen.

FIRST FOLIO VERSE NOTES:

This is a soliloquy: **See Note 25**.

The mid-line endings show his mood at first: **See Note 18**, 7 of them until the full stop and the end of a thought is finally at the end of a line: **See Note 2**.

There are also a large number of capitals worth looking at: **See Note 5**.

He addresses plural elements as 'you', but all singularities as 'thou': **See Note 22**.

There are some wonderful lists to consider, and as usual the order of them makes for insights into his attitude and mood: **See Note 14**.

'Some of sixteen' is changed in the Second Folio to 'Son of sixteen' — but 'some' can play just as well.

'generall Filthes' = common prostitutes; 'Bannes' = curses.

The Winters Tale, I-2

LEONTES

To your owne bents dispose you: you'le be found,
Be you beneath the Sky: I am angling now,
(Though you perceive me not how I give Lyne)
Goe too, goe too.
How she holds up the Neb? the Byll to him?
And armes her with the boldnesse of a Wife
To her allowing Husband. Gone already,
Inch-thick, knee-deepe; ore head and eares a fork'd one.
Goe play (Boy) play: thy Mother playes, and I
Play too; but so disgrac'd a part, whose issue
Will hisse me to my Grave: Contempt and Clamor
Will be my Knell. Goe play (Boy) play, there have been
(Or I am much deceiv'd) Cuckolds ere now,
And many a man there is (even at this present,
Now, while I speake this) holds his Wife by th'Arme,
That little thinkes she ha's been sluyc'd in's absence,
And his Pond fish'd by his next Neighbor (by
Sir *Smile*, his Neighbor:) nay, there's comfort in't,
Whiles other men have Gates, and those Gates open'd
(As mine) against their will.   Should all despaire
That have revolted Wives, the tenth of Mankind
Would hang themselves.   Physick for't, there's none:
It is a bawdy Planet, that will strike
Where 'tis predominant; and 'tis powrefull: thinke it:
From East, West, North, and South, be it concluded,
No Barricado for a Belly.   Know't,
It will let in and out the Enemy,
With bag and baggage: many thousand on's
Have the Disease, and feele't not.   How now Boy?

FIRST FOLIO VERSE NOTES:

This is a powerful soliloquy: **See Note 25**.

There is a significant half-line: **See Note 17**, begging for stage business.

The end words are particularly important: **See Note 9**, giving clarity to what he is saying.

There are a lot of capitalized words, mostly connected with his sexual jealousy: **See Note 5**.

The brackets play well if played differently: **See Note 16**.

There are a large number of contracted words 'in't; for't; on's; feele't' which give a jagged edge to the speech: **See Note 23**.

'Neb' = mouth.

The life and death of King John, II-1

BASTARD

Mad world, mad kings, mad composition:
John to stop *Arthurs* Title in the whole,
Hath willingly departed with a part,
And France, whose armour Conscience buckled on,
Whom zeale and charitie brought to the field,
As Gods owne souldier, rounded in the eare,
With that same purpose-changer, that slye divel,
That Broker, that still breakes the pate of faith,
That dayly breake-vow, he that winnes of all,
Of kings, of beggers, old men, yong men, maids,
Who having no externall thing to loose,
But the word Maid, cheats the poore Maide of that.
That smooth-fac'd Gentleman, tickling commoditie,
Commoditie, the byas of the world,
The world, who of it selfe is peysed well,
Made to run even, upon even ground;
Till this advantage, this vile drawing byas,
This sway of motion, this commoditie,
Makes it take head from all indifferency,
From all direction, purpose, course, intent.
And this same byas, this Commoditie,
This Bawd, this Broker, this all-changing-word,
Clap'd on the outward eye of fickle France,
Hath drawne him from his owne determin'd ayd,
From a resolv'd and honourable warre,
To a most base and vile-concluded peace.
And why rayle I on this Commoditie?
But for because he hath not wooed me yet:
Not that I have the power to clutch my hand,
When his faire Angels would salute my palme,

But for my hand, as unattempted yet,
Like a poore begger, raileth on the rich.
Well, whiles I am a begger, I will raile,
And say there is no sin but to be rich:
And being rich, my vertue then shall be,
To say there is no vice, but beggerie:
Since Kings breake faith upon commoditie,
Gaine be my Lord, for I will worship thee.

FIRST FOLIO VERSE NOTES:

A soliloquy for the Bastard: **See Note 25**.

The first line with its repetition of 'mad': **See Note 13** continues on for another 11 lines: **See Note 2**. There are then 6 repetitions of the word 'that'.

The word 'Commoditie' is used throughout, and the repetitious nature of the speech is shown by how often one line begins with the word used to end the previous one: **See Note 23**.

The assonances help show the direction of the speech, such as: 'departed/part/France/armour'; and 'breakes/pate/faith/daily/break-vow': **See Note 10**.

The list he uses is instructive: 'kings/beggers/old men/yong men/maids': **See Note 14**.

The piece ends with 2 rhyming couplets: **See Note 11**.

'peysed' = balanced.

The life and death of King John, III-2

JOHN

Good friend, thou hast no cause to say so yet,
But thou shalt have: and creepe time nere so slow,
Yet it shall come, for me to doe thee good.
I had a thing to say, but let it goe:
The Sunne is in the heaven, and the proud day,
Attended with the pleasures of the world,
Is all too wanton, and too full of gawdes
To give me audience: If the mid-night bell
Did with his iron tongue, and brazen mouth
Sound on into the drowzie race of night:
If this same were a Church-yard where we stand,
And thou possessed with a thousand wrongs:
Or if that surly spirit melancholy
Had bak'd thy bloud, and made it heavy, thicke,
Which else runnes tickling up and downe the veines,
Making that idiot laughter keepe mens eyes,
And straine their cheekes to idle merriment,
A passion hatefull to my purposes:
Or if that thou couldst see me without eyes,
Heare me without thine eares, and make reply
Without a tongue, using conceit alone,
Without eyes, eares, and harmefull sound of words:
Then, in despight of brooded watchfull day,
I would into thy bosome poure my thoughts:
But (ah) I will not, yet I love thee well,
And by my troth I thinke thou lov'st me well.

FIRST FOLIO VERSE NOTES:

The first 3 lines are one thought, and then there is a very long thought indeed: **See Note 2**.

Choosing the end word of each line helps being precise on the meaning of the speech: **See Note 9**.

The most significant repeated word is 'if' (4 times): **See Note 13**, together with 4 lots of 'without' (which culminate in a wonderful 'Then').

The ends of the last 2 lines being very similar should become part of the acting: **See Note 23**.

The life and death of King Richard the Second, II-1

GAUNT

Me thinkes I am a Prophet new inspir'd,
And thus expiring, do foretell of him,
His rash fierce blaze of Ryot cannot last,
For violent fires soone burne out themselves,
Small showres last long, but sodaine stormes are short,
He tyres betimes, that spurs too fast betimes;
With eager feeding, food doth choake the feeder:
Light vanity, insatiate cormorant,
Consuming meanes soone preyes upon it selfe.
This royall Throne of Kings, this sceptred Isle,
This earth of Majesty, this seate of Mars,
This other Eden, demy paradise,
This Fortresse built by Nature for her selfe,
Against infection, and the hand of warre:
This happy breed of men, this little world,
This precious stone, set in the silver sea,
Which serves it in the office of a wall,
Or as a Moate defensive to a house,
Against the envy of lesse happier Lands,
This blessed plot, this earth, this Realme, this England,
This Nurse, this teeming wombe of Royall Kings,
Fear'd by their breed, and famous for their birth,
Renowned for their deeds, as farre from home,
For Christian service, and true Chivalrie,
As is the sepulcher in stubborne *Jury*
Of the Worlds ransome, blessed *Maries* Sonne.
This Land of such deere soules, this deere-deere Land,
Deere for her reputation through the world,
Is now Leas'd out (I dye pronouncing it)

Like to a Tenement or pelting Farme.
England bound in with the triumphant sea,
Whose rocky shore beates backe the envious siedge
Of watery Neptune, is now bound in with shame,
With Inky blottes, and rotten Parchment bonds.
That England, that was wont to conquer others,
Hath made a shamefull conquest of it selfe.
Ah! would the scandall vanish with my life,
How happy then were my ensuing death?

FIRST FOLIO VERSE NOTES:

The speech is marked out by the constant repetition of the word 'this' (17 times): **See Note 13**, and a large clue needs a large acting solution. (Notice, however, a sudden 'that' towards the end of the speech): **See Note 23**.

The capitals all through the speech give it a dignity: **See Note 5**.

The alliterations and assonances point towards a large number of verbal conceits: **See Note 10**.

There is a 17 line thought, starting 'This royall Throne': **See Note 2** that builds to the phrase 'blessed *Maries* Sonne.'

There are some significant separations 'this sceptred'; 'this seate'; 'precious stone': 'envious siedge': **See Note 20**.

Make sure the speech ends not with a statement, but with the question so clearly marked.

'Jury' = Judea; 'pelting' = paltry.

The life and death of King Richard the Second, II-2

YORKE

Heav'n for his mercy, what a tide of woes
Come rushing on this wofull Land at once?
I know not what to do: I would to heaven
(So my untruth had not provok'd him to it)
The King had cut off my head with my brothers.
What, are there postes dispatcht for Ireland?
How shall we do for money for these warres?
Come sister (Cozen I would say) pray pardon me.
Go fellow, get thee home, provide some Carts,
And bring away the Armour that is there.
Gentlemen, will you muster men?
If I know how, or which way to order these affaires
Thus disorderly thrust into my hands,
Never beleeve me.   Both are my kinsmen,
Th'one is my Soveraigne, whom both my oath
And dutie bids defend: th'other againe
Is my kinsman, whom the King hath wrong'd,
Whom conscience, and my kindred bids to right:
Well, somewhat we must do: Come Cozen,
Ile dispose of you.   Gentlemen, go muster up your men,
And meet me presently at Barkley Castle:
I should to Plashy too: but time will not permit,
All is uneven, and every thing is left at six and seven.

FIRST FOLIO VERSE NOTES:

The first word in the Quarto versions was 'God', changed in the Folio to 'Heaven' under the anti-blasphemy ruling of the time.

There are 2 mid-line endings: **See Note 18**, which end the longer thoughts in the middle of the speech.

A number of lines are over-long, giving an unevenness to the whole speech: **See Note 17**.

There is a half-line: 'Gentlemen, will you muster men?', and the phrase being repeated later on, it gives a nice character slant to Yorke, culminating in his admission that 'every thing is left at six and seven': **See Note 23**.

The life and death of
King Richard the Second, III-2

RICHARD

No matter where; of comfort no man speake:
Let's talke of Graves, of Wormes, and Epitaphs,
Make Dust our Paper, and with Raynie eyes
Write Sorrow on the Bosome of the Earth.
Let's chuse Executors, and talke of Wills:
And yet not so; for what can we bequeath,
Save our deposed bodies to the ground?
Our Lands, our Lives, and all are *Bullingbrookes*,
And nothing can we call our owne, but Death,
And that small Modell of the barren Earth,
Which serves as Paste, and Cover to our Bones:
For Heavens sake let us sit upon the ground,
And tell sad stories of the death of Kings:
How some have been depos'd, some slaine in warre,
Some haunted by the Ghosts they have depos'd,
Some poyson'd by their Wives, some sleeping kill'd,
All murther'd. For within the hollow Crowne
That rounds the mortall Temples of a King,
Keepes Death his Court, and there the Antique sits
Scoffing his State, and grinning at his Pompe,
Allowing him a breath, a little Scene,
To Monarchize, be fear'd, and kill with lookes,
Infusing him with selfe and vaine conceit,
As if this Flesh, which walls about our Life,
Were Brasse impregnable: and humor'd thus,
Comes at the last, and with a little Pinne
Bores through his Castle Walls, and farwell King.
Cover your heads, and mock not flesh and blood
With solemne Reverence: throw away Respect,
Tradition, Forme, and Ceremonious dutie,
For you have but mistooke me all this while:

I live with Bread like you, feele Want,
Taste Griefe, need Friends: subjected thus,
How can you say to me, I am a King?

FIRST FOLIO VERSE NOTES:

It is essential not to end the first thought at the end of the first line — it is the opening part of a long argument, not a series of statements: **See Note 2**.

The mid-line ending in Line 17 stops the piece being maudlin, but drives the conclusion on: **See Note 18**.

The list 'Graves, Wormes, and Epitaphs' is a precise movement of thought, from the initial death, through what happens next (corruption) to the final epitaph (that probably no-one reads): **See Note 14**.

The capitals are their usual help in refining the sense of the speech: **See Note 5**.

The usual notice needs to be taken of the '-ed' endings to keep the meter going: **See Note 7**.

There is a good pun on 'subjected' at the end: **See Note 15**.

The Quarto, not restricted by the later anti blashemy laws, prints the 12th line as: 'For Gods sake let us sit upon the ground,'.

'Antique' = jester.

The life and death of King Richard the Second, III-3

RICHARD

What must the King doe now? must he submit?
The King shall doe it: Must he be depos'd?
The King shall be contented: Must he loose
The Name of King? o'Gods Name let it goe.
Ile give my Jewels for a sett of Beades,
My gorgeous Pallace, for a Hermitage,
My gay Apparrell, for an Almes-mans Gowne,
My figur'd Goblets, for a Dish of Wood,
My Scepter, for a Palmers walking Staffe,
My Subjects, for a payre of carved Saints,
And my large Kingdome, for a little Grave,
A little little Grave, an obscure Grave.
Or Ile be buryed in the Kings high-way,
Some way of common Trade, where Subjects feet
May howrely trample on their Soveraignes Head:
For on my heart they tread now, whilest I live;
And buryed once, why not upon my Head?
Aumerle, thou weep'st (my tender-hearted Cousin)
Wee'le make foule Weather with despised Teares:
Our sighes, and they, shall lodge the Summer Corne,
And make a Dearth in this revolting Land.
Or shall we play the Wantons with our Wocs,
And make some prettie Match, with shedding Teares?
As thus: to drop them still upon one place,
Till they have fretted us a payre of Graves,
Within the Earth: and therein lay'd, there lyes
Two Kinsmen, digg'd their Graves with weeping Eyes?
Would not this ill, doe well? Well, well, I see
I talke but idly, and you mock at mee.

Most mightie Prince, my Lord *Northumberland*,
What sayes King *Bullingbrooke*?   Will his Majestie
Give *Richard* leave to live, till *Richard* die?
You make a Legge, and *Bullingbrooke* sayes I.

FIRST FOLIO VERSE NOTES:

This speech has a long list of antithetical images, and the piling of each image on either side of an imaginary balance can really unlock the sense of the speech: **See Note 23**.

The repetition of the words 'King' and 'my' shape the sense: **See Note 13**.

Note the long spelling of 'mee': **See Note 6**.

He refers to his cousin Aumerle as 'thou', but the others as 'you': **See Note 22**.

There is a nursery-style rhyme of 'see/mee', and it all ends with a rhyming couplets: **See Note 11**.

'Palmers' = pilgrim's.

The life and death of
King Richard the Second, V-4

KING RICHARD

I have bin studying, how to compare
This Prison where I live, unto the World:
And for because the world is populous,
And heere is not a Creature, but my selfe,
I cannot do it: yet Ile hammer't out.
My Braine, Ile prove the Female to my Soule,
My Soule, the Father: and these two beget
A generation of still breeding Thoughts;
And these same Thoughts, people this Little World
In humors, like the people of this world,
For no thought is contented.   The better sort,
As thoughts of things Divine, are intermixt
With scruples, and do set the Faith it selfe
Against the Faith: as thus: Come litle ones: and then again,
It is as hard to come, as for a Camell
To thred the posterne of a Needles eye.
Thoughts tending to Ambition, they do plot
Unlikely wonders; how these vaine weake nailes
May teare a passage through the Flinty ribbes
Of this hard world, my ragged prison walles:
And for they cannot, dye in their owne pride.
Thoughts tending to Content, flatter themselves,
That they are not the first of Fortunes slaves,
Nor shall not be the last.   Like silly Beggars,
Who sitting in the Stockes, refuge their shame
That many have, and others must sit there;
And in this Thought, they finde a kind of ease,
Bearing their owne misfortune on the backe
Of such as have before indur'd the like.

Thus play I in one Prison, many people,
And none contented.   Sometimes am I King;
Then Treason makes me wish my selfe a Beggar,
And so I am.   Then crushing penurie,
Perswades me, I was better when a King:
Then am I king'd againe: and by and by,
Thinke that I am un-king'd by *Bullingbrooke*,
And straight am nothing.   But what ere I am,

MUSICK.

Nor I, nor any man, that but man is,
With nothing shall be pleas'd, till he be eas'd
With being nothing.   Musicke do I heare?
Ha, ha? keepe time: How sowre sweet Musicke is,
When Time is broke, and no Proportion kept?
So is it in the Musicke of mens lives:
And heere have I the daintinesse of eare,
To heare time broke in a disorder'd string:
But for the Concord of my State and Time,
Had not an eare to heare my true Time broke.
I wasted Time, and now doth Time waste me:
For now hath Time made me his numbring clocke;
My Thoughts, are minutes; and with Sighes they jarre,
Their watches on unto mine eyes, the outward Watch,
Whereto my finger, like a Dialls point,
Is pointing still, in cleansing them from teares.
Now sir, the sound that tels what houre it is,
Are clamorous groanes, that strike upon my heart,
Which is the bell: so Sighes, and Teares, and Grones,
Shew Minutes, Houres, and Times: but my Time
Runs poasting on, in *Bullingbrookes* proud joy,
While I stand fooling heere, his jacke o'th'Clocke.
This Musicke mads me, let it sound no more,
For though it have holpe madmen to their wits,
In me it seemes, it will make wise-men mad:

Yet blessing on his heart that gives it me;
For 'tis a signe of love, and love to *Richard*,
Is a strange Brooch, in this all-hating world.

FIRST FOLIO VERSE NOTES:

The temptation to become maudlin and sentimental with this speech is carefully tempered by the 6 mid-line endings, that drive the whole on: **See Note 18**.

It is a soliloquy, and the full theatricality of Richard is exposed as he chats to the audience: **See Note 25**.

There is a long line 'Against the Faith: as thus: Come litle ones: and then again': **See Note 17**.

The capitals provide their usual help: **See Note 5**, as do the separations: **See Note 20**.

There are a lot of words repeated: **See Note 13**, and the end word of each line is, as usual, significant: **See Note 9**.

The First Part of Henry the Fourth, I-2

PRINCE HAL

I know you all, and will a-while uphold
The unyoak'd humor of your idlenesse:
Yet heerein will I imitate the Sunne,
Who doth permit the base contagious cloudes
To smother up his Beauty from the world,
That when he please againe to be himselfe,
Being wanted, he may be more wondred at,
By breaking through the foule and ugly mists
Of vapours, that did seeme to strangle him.
If all the yeare were playing holidaies,
To sport, would be as tedious as to worke;
But when they seldome come, they wisht-for come,
And nothing pleaseth but rare accidents.
So when this loose behaviour I throw off,
And pay the debt I never promised;
By how much better then my word I am,
By so much shall I falsifie mens hopes,
And like bright Mettall on a sullen ground:
My reformation glittering o're my fault,
Shall shew more goodly, and attract more eyes,
Then that which hath no soyle to set it off.
Ile so offend, to make offence a skill,
Redeeming time, when men thinke least I will.

FIRST FOLIO VERSE NOTES:

The first 9 lines are all one thought: **<u>See Note 2</u>**.

There is the obvious pun on 'Sunne' (the heavenly body and himself the child of his father): **<u>See Note 15</u>**, as well as word play on 'offend' and 'offence' — showing that there is a conscious playfulness in the speaker.

The repetitions of 'much' and of 'by' also add to the mood and attitude: **<u>See Note 13</u>**.

The '-ed' in promised is needed to keep the meter going: **<u>See Note 7</u>**.

The repetition of 2 lines starting with 'By' and the word 'more' help end the speech nicely: **<u>See Note 13</u>**.

Editors often choose 'foyle' instead of 'soyle' in the 3rd line from the end.

The First Part of Henry the Fourth, I-3

HOTSPURRE

My Liege, I did deny no Prisoners.
But, I remember when the fight was done,
When I was dry with Rage, and extreame Toyle,
Breathlesse, and Faint, leaning upon my Sword,
Came there a certaine Lord, neat and trimly drest;
Fresh as a Bride-groome, and his Chin new reapt,
Shew'd like a stubble Land at Harvest home.
He was perfumed like a Milliner,
And 'twixt his Finger and his Thumbe, he held
A Pouncet-box: which ever and anon
He gave his Nose, and took't away againe:
Who therewith angry, when it next came there,
Tooke it in Snuffe.   And still he smil'd and talk'd:
And as the Souldiers bare dead bodies by,
He call'd them untaught Knaves, Unmannerly,
To bring a slovenly unhandsome Coarse
Betwixt the Winde, and his Nobility.
With many Holiday and Lady tearme
He question'd me: Among the rest, demanded
My Prisoners, in your Majesties behalfe.
I then, all-smarting, with my wounds being cold,
(To be so pestered with a Popingay)
Out of my Greefe, and my Impatience,
Answer'd (neglectingly) I know not what,
He should, or should not: For he made me mad,
To see him shine so briske, and smell so sweet,
To talke so like a Waiting-Gentlewoman,
Of Guns, and Drums, and Wounds: God save the marke;
And telling me, the Soveraign'st thing on earth
Was Parmacity, for an inward bruise:
And that it was great pitty, so it was,
That villanous Salt-peter should be digg'd

Out of the Bowels of the harmlesse Earth,
Which many a good Tall Fellow had destroy'd
So Cowardly.   And but for these vile Gunnes,
He would himselfe have beene a Souldier.
This bald, unjoynted Chat of his (my Lord)
Made me to answer indirectly (as I said.)
And I beseech you, let not this report
Come currant for an Accusation,
Betwixt my Love, and your high Majesty.

FIRST FOLIO VERSE NOTES:

The speaker starts off calling the listener 'My Liege', and then goes on to address him as 'your Majesty'; 'my Lord' and finally 'your high Majesty': **See Note 22**.

It is important to end the first thought at the end of the first line, and start off the second line (and thought) with a 'But'.

The mid-line endings add drive and force to the speech: **See Note 18**, and the colons keep the argument clear: **See Note 3**.

The '-ed' endings in such as 'perfumed' need to be used to keep the meter going: **See Note 7**.

The alliteration of 'beare dead bodies by' gives the attitude to this part of the speech: **See Note 10**.

The capitals (especially of 'Chat') point up the meaning and mood: **See Note 5**.

The First Part of Henry the Fourth, III-2

PRINCE HAL

Doe not thinke so, you shall not finde it so:
And Heaven forgive them, that so much have sway'd
Your Majesties good thoughts away from me:
I will redeeme all this on *Percies* head,
And in the closing of some glorious day,
Be bold to tell you, that I am your Sonne,
When I will weare a Garment all of Blood,
And staine my favours in a bloody Maske:
Which washt away, shall scowre my shame with it.
And that shall be the day, when ere it lights,
That this same Child of Honor and Renowne,
This gallant *Hotspur*, this all-praysed Knight,
And your unthought-of *Harry* chance to meet:
For every Honor sitting on his Helme,
Would they were multitudes, and on my head
My shames redoubled.   For the time will come,
That I shall make this Northerne Youth exchange
His glorious Deedes for my Indignities:
Percy is but my Factor, good my Lord,
To engrosse up glorious Deedes on my behalfe:
And I will call him to so strict account,
That he shall render every Glory up,
Yea, even the sleightest worship of his time,
Or I will teare the Reckoning from his Heart.
This, in the Name of Heaven, I promise here:
The which, if I performe, and doe survive,
I doe beseech your Majestie, may salve
The long-growne Wounds of my intemperature:
If not, the end of Life cancells all Bands,

And I will dye a hundred thousand Deaths,
Ere breake the smallest parcell of this Vow.

FIRST FOLIO VERSE NOTES:

The first 9 lines are all one thought: **See Note 2**, and it is important not to end the first line as if it were one thought.

The repetitions of 'so' need to be acknowledged: **See Note 13**.

There is one nice mid-line ending: **See Note 18**.

The Prince makes interesting changes in the way he refers to his rival, starting with Percy, going on to Hotspur, then Northern Youth, and ending up with Percy again: **See Note 22.**

'Factor' = agent.

The Second Part of Henry the Fourth, III-1

KING HENRY

Goe call the Earles of Surrey, and of Warwicke:
But ere they come, bid them ore-reade these Letters,
And well consider of them: make good speed.

EXIT PAGE.

How many thousand of my poorest Subjects
Are at this howre asleepe?   O Sleepe, O gentle Sleepe,
Natures soft Nurse, how have I frighted thee,
That thou no more wilt weigh my eye-lids downe,
And steepe my Sences in Forgetfulnesse?
Why rather (Sleepe) lyest thou in smoakie Cribs,
Upon uneasie Pallads stretching thee,
And huisht with bussing Night, flyes to thy slumber,
Then in the perfum'd Chambers of the Great?
Under the Canopies of costly State,
And lull'd with sounds of sweetest Melodie?
O thou dull God, why lyest thou with the vilde,
In loathsome Beds, and leav'st the Kingly Couch,
A Watch-case, or a common Larum-Bell?
Wilt thou, upon the high and giddie Mast,
Seale up the Ship-boyes Eyes, and rock his Braines,
In Cradle of the rude imperious Surge,
And in the visitation of the Windes,
Who take the Ruffian Billowes by the top,
Curling their monstrous heads, and hanging them
With deaff'ning Clamors in the slipp'ry Clouds,
That with the hurley, Death it selfe awakes?
Canst thou (O partiall Sleepe) give thy Repose
To the wet Sea-Boy, in an houre so rude:

And in the calmest, and most stillest Night,
With all appliances, and meanes to boote,
Deny it to a King?   Then happy Lowe, lye downe,
Uneasie lyes the Head, that weares a Crowne.

FIRST FOLIO VERSE NOTES:

This is a soliloquy: **See Note 25**, where the fourth line has a feminine ending, and the next one is an Alexandrine: **See Note 9**.

The capitals all through are very useful: **See Note 5**.

The word 'Sleepe' is put into brackets: **See Note 16**.

There are also the single 'O's': **See Note 12**.

The repeated word 'Sleepe', the heavy use of alliteration and assonance give mood to the piece: **See Note 10**.

Editors change 'give thy Repose' to 'give them Repose'.

'Lowe' = lowly ones.

The Second Part of Henry the Fourth, IV-2

PRINCE HENRY

O pardon me (my Liege)
But for my Teares,
The most Impediments unto my Speech,
I had fore-stall'd this deere, and deepe Rebuke,
Ere you (with greefe) had spoke, and I had heard
The course of it so farre.   There is your Crowne,
And he that weares the Crowne immortally,
Long guard it yours.   If I affect it more,
Then as your Honour, and as your Renowne,
Let me no more from this Obedience rise,
Which my most true, and inward duteous Spirit
Teacheth this prostrate, and exteriour bending.
Heaven witnesse with me, when I heere came in,
And found no course of breath within your Majestie,
How cold it strooke my heart.   If I do faine,
O let me, in my present wildenesse, dye,
And never live, to shew th'incredulous World,
The Noble change that I have purposed.
Comming to looke on you, thinking you dead,
(And dead almost (my Liege) to thinke you were)
I spake unto the Crowne (as having sense)
And thus upbraided it.   The Care on thee depending,
Hath fed upon the body of my Father,
Therefore, thou best of Gold, art worst of Gold.
Other, lesse fine in Charract, is more precious,
Preserving life, in Med'cine potable:
But thou, most Fine, most Honour'd, most Renown'd,
Hast eate the Bearer up.
Thus (my Royall Liege)

Accusing it, I put it on my Head,
To try with it (as with an Enemie,
That had before my face murdred my Father)
The Quarrell of a true Inheritor.
But if it did infect my blood with Joy,
Or swell my Thoughts, to any straine of Pride,
If any Rebell, or vaine spirit of mine,
Did, with the least Affection of a Welcome,
Give entertainment to the might of it,
Let heaven, for ever, keepe it from my head,
And make me, as the poorest Vassaile is,
That doth with awe, and terror kneele to it.

FIRST FOLIO VERSE NOTES:

The half-lines are important (especially since the editors would have removed them from their versions): **See Note 17**.

There are a lot of mid-line endings (4) which add urgency: **See Note 18**.

The speaker addresses his father as 'you', but the crown as 'thee': **See Note 22**.

There are a lot of brackets used in this speech (even a bracket within a bracket): **See Note 16**.

He refers to his father successively as 'Liege/Majestie/ Liege/Father/Liege/Father': **See Note 22**, and that should be enough to spur any performer.

Editors change 'most Impediments' to 'moist Impediments'.

The Life of Henry the Fift, Prologue

PROLOGUE

O For a Muse of Fire, that would ascend
The brightest Heaven of Invention:
A Kingdome for a Stage, Princes to Act,
And Monarchs to behold the swelling Scene.
Then should the Warlike *Harry*, like himselfe,
Assume the Port of *Mars*, and at his heeles
(Leasht in, like Hounds) should Famine, Sword, and Fire
Crouch for employment.   But pardon, Gentles all:
The flat unraysed Spirits, that hath dar'd,
On this unworthy Scaffold, to bring forth
So great an Object.   Can this Cock-Pit hold
The vastie fields of France?   Or may we cramme
Within this Woodden O, the very Caskes
That did affright the Ayre at Agincourt?
O pardon: since a crooked Figure may
Attest in little place a Million,
And let us, Cyphers to this great Accompt,
On your imaginarie Forces worke.
Suppose within the Girdle of these Walls
Are now confin'd two mightie Monarchies,
Whose high, up-reared, and abutting Fronts,
The perillous narrow Ocean parts asunder.
Peece out our imperfections with your thoughts:
Into a thousand parts divide one Man,
And make imaginarie Puissance.
Thinke when we talke of Horses, that you see them,
Printing their prowd Hoofes i'th'receiving Earth:
For 'tis your thoughts that now must deck our Kings,
Carry them here and there: Jumping o're Times;
Turning th'accomplishment of many yeeres
Into an Howre-glasse: for the which supplie,
Admit me *Chorus* to this Historie;

Who Prologue-like, your humble patience pray,
Gently to heare, kindly to judge our Play.

FIRST FOLIO VERSE NOTES:

This is a soliloquy: **See Note 25**, and it starts with a single 'O': **See Note 12** (although the 'Woodden O' refers to the Globe Theatre itself).

There are 3 important mid-line endings: **See Note 18**.

The sense of the speech is contained by *not* putting a full stop after the second line: **See Note 2**, and by carefully choosing the end words, especially on the first line: **See Note 9**.

The colons in the speech are of particular help: **See Note 3**.

The '-ed' endings need to be used: **See Note 7**.

There is a sudden gear change back to simple language after the flowery beginning: **See Note 21**.

'Port' = demeanor; 'Puissance' = troops.

The Life of Henry the Fift, II-Prologue

CHORUS

Thus with imagin'd wing our swift Scene flyes,
In motion of no lesse celeritie then that of Thought.
Suppose, that you have seene
The well-appointed King at Dover Peer,
Embarke his Royaltie: and his brave Fleet,
With silken Streamers, the young *Phebus* fayning;
Play with your Fancies: and in them behold,
Upon the Hempen Tackle, Ship-boyes climbing;
Heare the shrill Whistle, which doth order give
To sounds confus'd: behold the threaden Sayles,
Borne with th'invisible and creeping Wind,
Draw the huge Bottomes through the furrowed Sea,
Bresting the loftie Surge. O, doe but thinke
You stand upon the Rivage, and behold
A Citie on th' inconstant Billowes dauncing:
For so appeares this Fleet Majesticall,
Holding due course to Harflew. Follow, follow:
Grapple your minds to sternage of this Navie,
And leave your England as dead Mid-night, still,
Guarded with Grandsires, Babyes, and old Women,
Eyther past, or not arriv'd to pyth and puissance:
For who is he, whose Chin is but enricht
With one appearing Hayre, that will not follow
These cull'd and choyse-drawne Cavaliers to France?
Worke, worke your Thoughts, and therein see a Siege:
Behold the Ordenance on their Carriages,
With fatall mouthes gaping on girded Harflew.
Suppose th'Embassador from the French comes back:
Tells *Harry*, That the King doth offer him
Katherine his Daughter, and with her to Dowrie,

Some petty and unprofitable Dukedomes.
The offer likes not: and the nimble Gunner
With Lynstock now the divellish Cannon touches,

ALARUM, AND CHAMBERS GOE OFF.

And downe goes all before them.   Still be kind,
And eech out our performance with your mind.

FIRST FOLIO VERSE NOTES:

This is a soliloquy: **See Note 25**.

The 2nd line is very long, and the 3rd a half-line. Editors mistakenly 'regularise' these 2 lines, but the acting note from the Folio is to cram the second line, and to pause before the third: **See Note 17**.

The lengths of all the thoughts are precise, and important to acknowledge: **See Note 2**.

There is a good single 'O': **See Note 12**.

The mid-line endings tell where the pressure is to be maintained in the speech: **See Note 18**.

There is a nice rhyming couplet to end the speech: **See Note 11**.

Editors change 'Dover' to 'Hampton'; and 'fayning' to 'fanning'.

'Rivage' = shore.

The Life of Henry the Fift, II-1

KING HENRY

Once more unto the Breach,
Deare friends, once more;
Or close the Wall up with our English dead:
In Peace, there's nothing so becomes a man,
As modest stillnesse, and humilitie:
But when the blast of Warre blowes in our eares,
Then imitate the action of the Tyger:
Stiffen the sinewes, commune up the blood,
Disguise faire Nature with hard-favour'd Rage:
Then lend the Eye a terrible aspect:
Let it pry through the portage of the Head,
Like the Brasse Cannon: let the Brow o'rewhelme it,
As fearefully, as doth a galled Rocke
O're-hang and jutty his confounded Base,
Swill'd with the wild and wastfull Ocean.
Now set the Teeth, and stretch the Nosthrill wide,
Hold hard the Breath, and bend up every Spirit
To his full height. On, on, you Noblish English,
Whose blood is fet from Fathers of Warre-proofe:
Fathers, that like so many *Alexanders*,
Have in these parts from Morne till Even fought,
And sheath'd their Swords, for lack of argument.
Dishonour not your Mothers: now attest,
That those whom you call'd Fathers, did beget you.
Be Coppy now to me of grosser blood,
And teach them how to Warre. And you good Yeomen,
Whose Lyms were made in England; shew us here
The mettell of your Pasture: let us sweare,
That you are worth your breeding: which I doubt not:
For there is none of you so meane and base,

That hath not Noble luster in your eyes.
I see you stand like Grey-hounds in the slips,
Straying upon the Start.   The Game's afoot:
Follow your Spirit; and upon this Charge,
Cry, God for *Harry*, England, and Saint *George*.

FIRST FOLIO VERSE NOTES:

The speech starts with 2 half-lines: **See Note 17** (inconveniently removed by all editors).

The first long thought goes all the way to 'Ocean': **See Note 2**, be particularly careful not to put a full stop after 'English dead:'.

The separation gives a care to beginning of the speech: 'modest stillnesse': **See Note 20**, which contrasts to the drive of the speech as the mid-line endings start kicking in: **See Note 18**.

'Straying upon the Start.' is the Folio and Quarto phrase — a precise description of a crowd anxious to get started.

He refers to the soldiers he is addressing progressively as 'Deare friends/Noblish English/Yeomen/Grey-hounds': **See Note 22**.

The changes between this version and the edited ones are the differences between a playing text, and a literary one.

Editors change 'commune up the blood' to 'conjure up the blood'; 'you Noblish English' to 'you noblest English'; 'Be Coppy now to me' to 'Be Coppy now to men'; and 'Straying upon the Start' to 'Straining upon the Start'.

The Life of Henry the Fift, III-Prologue

CHORUS

Now entertaine conjecture of a time,
When creeping Murmure and the poring Darke
Fills the wide Vessell of the Universe.
From Camp to Camp, through the foule Womb of Night
The Humme of eyther Army stilly sounds;
That the fixt Centinels almost receive
The secret Whispers of each others Watch.
Fire answers fire, and through their paly flames
Each Battaile sees the others umber'd face.
Steed threatens Steed, in high and boastfull Neighs
Piercing the Nights dull Eare: and from the Tents,
The Armourers accomplishing the Knights,
With busie Hammers closing Rivets up,
Give dreadfull note of preparation.
The Countrey Cocks doe crow, the Clocks doe towle:
And the third howre of drowsie Morning nam'd,
Prowd of their Numbers, and secure in Soule,
The confident and over-lustie French,
Doe the low-rated English play at Dice;
And chide the creeple-tardy-gated Night,
Who like a foule and ougly Witch doth limpe
So tediously away.   The poore condemned English,
Like Sacrifices, by their watchfull Fires
Sit patiently, and inly ruminate
The Mornings danger: and their gesture sad,
Investing lanke-leane Cheekes, and Warre-worne Coats,
Presented them unto the gazing Moone
So many horride Ghosts.   O now, who will behold
The Royall Captaine of this ruin'd Band
Walking from Watch to Watch, from Tent to Tent;
Let him cry, Prayse and Glory on his head:
For forth he goes, and visits all his Hoast,

Bids them good morrow with a modest Smyle,
And calls them Brothers, Friends, and Countreymen.
Upon his Royall Face there is no note,
How dread an Army hath enrounded him;
Nor doth he dedicate one jot of Colour
Unto the wearie and all-watched Night:
But freshly lookes, and over-beares Attaint,
With chearefull semblance, and sweet Majestie:
That every Wretch, pining and pale before,
Beholding him, plucks comfort from his Lookes.
A Largesse universall, like the Sunne,
His liberall Eye doth give to every one,
Thawing cold feare, that meane and gentle all
Behold, as may unworthinesse define.
A little touch of *Harry* in the Night,
And so our Scene must to the Battaile flye:
Where, O for pitty, we shall much disgrace,
With foure or five most vile and ragged foyles,
(Right ill dispos'd, in brawle ridiculous)
The Name of Agincourt: Yet sit and see,
Minding true things, by what their Mock'ries bee.

FIRST FOLIO VERSE NOTES:

As with all soliloquies: **See Note 25**, the arguments and structure of the speech are carefully defined by the lengths of thought: **See Note 2**.

It is also illuminated by which words end each line: **See Note 9**.

The assonances and alliterations 'Whispers/Watch'; 'paly/flames' give intimacy to the speech: **See Note 10**.

There are 2 single 'O''s to play with: **See Note 12**.

The traditional editors put 'A little touch of *Harry* in the Night,' at the end of the previous thought; here in the Folio it is the start of a new thought, and it plays beautifully: **See Note 4**.

The Life of Henry the Fift, III-1

KING HENRY

Upon the King, let us our Lives, our Soules,
Our Debts, our carefull Wives,
Our Children, and our Sinnes, lay on the King:
We must beare all.
O hard Condition, Twin-borne with Greatnesse,
Subject to the breath of every foole, whose sence,
No more can feele, but his owne wringing.
What infinite hearts-ease must Kings neglect,
That private men enjoy?
And what have Kings, that Privates have not too,
Save Ceremonie, save generall Ceremonie?
And what art thou, thou Idoll Ceremonie?
What kind of God art thou? that suffer'st more
Of mortall griefes, then doe thy worshippers.
What are thy Rents? what are thy Commings in?
O Ceremonie, shew me but thy worth.
What? is thy Soule of Odoration?
Art thou ought else but Place, Degree, and Forme,
Creating awe and feare in other men?
Wherein thou art lesse happy, being fear'd,
Then they in fearing.
What drink'st thou oft, in stead of Homage sweet,
But poyson'd flatterie? O, be sick, great Greatnesse,
And bid thy Ceremonie give thee cure.
Thinks thou the fierie Fever will goe out
With Titles blowne from Adulation?
Will it give place to flexure and low bending?
Canst thou, when thou command'st the beggers knee,
Command the health of it? No, thou prowd Dreame,
That play'st so subtilly with a Kings Repose.
I am a King that find thee.

FIRST FOLIO VERSE NOTES:

This is a soliloquy for King Henry: **See Note 25**.

The consistent use of half-lines stops the flow, and gives a stop start rhythm to the speech: **See Note 17**; (even the editors cannot 'regularise' all the half-lines away, though they do get rid of some).

'Ceremonie' is repeated 5 times, and 'O' 3 times: **See Notes 12 & 13**.

There are 2 mid-line endings (ending in a question mark) towards the end of the speech: **See Note 18**.

The whole ends with a simple statement: **See Note 21**, although in the Folio the speech continues for another 25 lines.

Editors change 'Soule of Odoration' to 'Soule of adoration'.

The third Part of Henry the Sixt, I-4

YORKE

Shee-Wolfe of France,
But worse then Wolves of France,
Whose Tongue more poysons then the Adders Tooth:
How ill-beseeming is it in thy Sex,
To triumph like an Amazonian Trull,
Upon their Woes, whom Fortune captivates?
But that thy Face is Vizard-like, unchanging,
Made impudent with use of evill deedes.
I would assay, prowd Queene, to make thee blush.
To tell thee whence thou cam'st, of whom deriv'd,
Were shame enough, to shame thee,
Wert thou not shamelesse.
Thy Father beares the type of King of Naples,
Of both Sicils, and Jerusalem,
Yet not so wealthie as an English Yeoman.
Hath that poore Monarch taught thee to insult?
It needes not, nor it bootes thee not, prowd Queene,
Unlesse the Adage must be verify'd,
That Beggers mounted, runne their Horse to death.
'Tis Beautie that doth oft make Women prowd,
But God he knowes, thy share thereof is small.
'Tis Vertue, that doth make them most admir'd,
The contrary, doth make thee wondred at.
'Tis Government that makes them seeme Divine,
The want thereof, makes thee abhominable.
Thou art as opposite to every good,
As the *Antipodes* are unto us,
Or as the South to the *Septentrion*.
Oh Tygres Heart, wrapt in a Womans Hide,
How could'st thou drayne the Life-blood of the Child,
To bid the Father wipe his eyes withall,
And yet be seene to beare a Womans face?

Women are soft, milde, pittifull, and flexible;
Thou, sterne, obdurate, flintie, rough, remorselesse.
Bidst thou me rage? why now thou hast thy wish.
Would'st have me weepe? why now thou hast thy will.
For raging Wind blowes up incessant showers,
And when the Rage allayes, the Raine begins.
These Teares are my sweet *Rutlands* Obsequies,
And every drop cryes vengeance for his death,
'Gainst thee fell *Clifford*, and thee false French-woman.

FIRST FOLIO VERSE NOTES:

The speech starts with 2 half-lines: **See Note 17**, and proceeds on with a lot of very short thoughts (and another 2 half-lines, run on by editors).

The 3 attacks each starting with ''Tis' give a nice build: **See Note 14**, as well as the lists of attributes and rudeness about women.

The build of alliterations on 'Would'st/weepe/why/will/Wind' add to the speaker's attitude: **See Note 10**.

Towards the end is a delicious pun on the word 'Raine' with both the wet and ruling meanings: **See Note 15**.

'bootes' = profits; 'Septentrion' = north.

The third Part of Henry the Sixt, II-4

KING HENRY

This battell fares like to the mornings Warre,
When dying clouds contend, with growing light,
What time the Shepheard blowing of his nailes,
Can neither call it perfect day, nor night.
Now swayes it this way, like a Mighty Sea,
Forc'd by the Tide, to combat with the Winde:
Now swayes it that way, like the selfe-same Sea,
Forc'd to retyre by furie of the Winde.
Sometime, the Flood prevailes; and than the Winde:
Now, one the better: then, another best;
Both tugging to be Victors, brest to brest:
Yet neither Conqueror, nor Conquered.
So is the equall poise of this fell Warre.
Heere on this Mole-hill will I sit me downe,
To whom God will, there be the Victorie:
For *Margaret* my Queene, and *Clifford* too
Have chid me from the Battell: Swearing both,
They prosper best of all when I am thence.
Would I were dead, if Gods good will were so;
For what is in this world, but Greefe and Woe.
Oh God! me thinkes it were a happy life,
To be no better then a homely Swaine,
To sit upon a hill, as I do now,
To carve out Dialls queintly, point by point,
Thereby to see the Minutes how they runne:
How many makes the Houre full compleate,
How many Houres brings about the Day,
How many Dayes will finish up the Yeare,
How many Yeares, a Mortall man may live.
When this is knowne, then to divide the Times:

So many Houres, must I tend my Flocke;
So many Houres, must I take my Rest:
So many Houres, must I Contemplate:
So many Houres, must I Sport my selfe:
So many Dayes, my Ewes have bene with yong:
So many weekes, ere the poore Fooles will Eane:
So many yeares, ere I shall sheere the Fleece:
So Minutes, Houres, Dayes, Monthes, and Yeares,
Past over to the end they were created,
Would bring white haires, unto a Quiet grave.

FIRST FOLIO VERSE NOTES:

As the King watches the battle from afar, he delivers this soliloquy: **See Note 25**.

There are 4 'How many''s and 7 'So many''s — a gift for building and noticing the direction of a list: **See Notes 13 & 14**.

There are a lot of short thoughts in this piece, and a lot of colons to provide the logic of the argument: **See Note 3**.

'So is the equall poise of this fell Warre.' is a statement all by itself.

There is a nice little rhyming couplet right in the middle 'so/ Woe': **See Note 11**.

The speech continues in the Folio for another 14 lines.

'Eane' = bring forth.

The Tragedy of Richard the Third, I-1

RICHARD

Now is the Winter of our Discontent,
Made glorious Summer by this Son of Yorke:
And all the clouds that lowr'd upon our house
In the deepe bosome of the Ocean buried.
Now are our browes bound with Victorious Wreathes,
Our bruised armes hung up for Monuments;
Our sterne Alarums chang'd to merry Meetings;
Our dreadfull Marches, to delightfull Measures.
Grim-visag'd Warre, hath smooth'd his wrinkled Front:
And now, in stead of mounting Barbed Steeds,
To fright the Soules of fearfull Adversaries,
He capers nimbly in a Ladies Chamber,
To the lascivious pleasing of a Lute.
But I, that am not shap'd for sportive trickes,
Nor made to court an amorous Looking-glasse:
I, that am Rudely stampt, and want loves Majesty,
To strut before a wonton ambling Nymph:
I, that am curtail'd of this faire Proportion,
Cheated of Feature by dissembling Nature,
Deform'd, un-finish'd, sent before my time
Into this breathing World, scarse halfe made up,
And that so lamely and unfashionable,
That dogges barke at me, as I halt by them.
Why I (in this weake piping time of Peace)
Have no delight to passe away the time,
Unlesse to see my Shadow in the Sunne,
And descant on mine owne Deformity.
And therefore, since I cannot prove a Lover,
To entertaine these faire well spoken dayes,
I am determined to prove a Villaine,

And hate the idle pleasures of these dayes.
Plots have I laide, Inductions dangerous,
By drunken Prophesies, Libels, and Dreames,
To set my Brother *Clarence* and the King
In deadly hate, the one against the other:
And if King *Edward* be as true and just,
As I am Subtle, False, and Treacherous,
This day should *Clarence* closely be mew'd up:
About a Prophesie, which sayes that G,
Of *Edwards* heyres the murtherer shall be.
Dive thoughts downe to my soule, here *Clarence* comes.

FIRST FOLIO VERSE NOTES:

This soliloquy: **See Note 25** starts with a bold 'Now',
and this is followed up in the speech with the sequence
'Now/now/But I/Why I', a wonderful pattern for the
speech: **See Note 26**, as does the build on the very
word 'I': **See Note 13**.

The separations 'glorious Summer' and 'this Son' near the
beginning give a care to the start of the piece: **See Note
20**.

There are a large amount of alliterations and assonances,
all contributing to a rich texture: **See Note 10**.

The end of the speech is a series of facts rattled off, once
the argument of the speech has been made: **See Note 21**.

'Measures' = dances; 'mew'd' = caged.

The Tragedy of Richard the Third, I-2

RICHARD

Was ever woman in this humour woo'd?
Was ever woman in this humour wonne?
Ile have her, but I will not keepe her long.
What? I that kill'd her Husband, and his Father,
To take her in her hearts extreamest hate,
With curses in her mouth, Teares in her eyes,
The bleeding witnesse of my hatred by,
Having God, her Conscience, and these bars against me,
And I, no Friends to backe my suite withall,
But the plaine Divell, and dissembling lookes?
And yet to winne her?   All the world to nothing.
Hah!
Hath she forgot alreadie that brave Prince,
Edward, her Lord, whom I (some three monthes since)
Stab'd in my angry mood, at Tewkesbury?
A sweeter, and a lovelier Gentleman,
Fram'd in the prodigallity of Nature:
Yong, Valiant, Wise, and (no doubt) right Royal,
The spacious World cannot againe affoord:
And will she yet abase her eyes on me,
That cropt the Golden prime of this sweet Prince,
And made her Widdow to a wofull Bed?
On me, whose All not equals *Edwards* Moytie?
On me, that halts, and am mishapen thus?
My Dukedome, to a Beggerly denier!
I do mistake my person all this while:
Upon my life she findes (although I cannot)
My selfe to be a marv'llous proper man.
Ile be at Charges for a Looking-glasse,
And entertaine a score or two of Taylors,

To study fashions to adorne my body:
Since I am crept in favour with my selfe,
I will maintaine it with some little cost.
But first Ile turne yon Fellow in his Grave,
And then returne lamenting to my Love.
Shine out faire Sunne, till I have bought a glasse,
That I may see my Shadow as I passe.

FIRST FOLIO VERSE NOTES:

Another soliloquy for Richard: **See Note 25**.

The first 7 words are the same for the first 2 lines — so they must be chosen to be repeated: **See Note 13**. Later on 'On me' is repeated twice as well, and the speaker uses the word 'I' a great deal: **See Note 23**.

There is a wonderful half-line with the one word 'Hah!': **See Note 17**.

The capitals in the speech all help towards understanding the speaker's attitude and mood: **See Note 5**, as well as all the alliterations and assonances: **See Note 10**.

The whole ends with a charming rhyming couplet: **See Note 11**.

'*Edwards* Moytie' = half of Edward; 'denier' = small copper coin.

The Tragedy of Richard the Third, I-4

CLARENCE

O, I have past a miserable night,
So full of fearefull Dreames, of ugly sights,
That as I am a Christian faithfull man,
I would not spend another such a night
Though 'twere to buy a world of happy daies:
So full of dismall terror was the time.

(*What was your dream my Lord, I pray you tel me*)

Me thoughts that I had broken from the Tower,
And was embark'd to crosse to Burgundy,
And in my company my Brother Glouster,
Who from my Cabin tempted me to walke,
Upon the Hatches: There we look'd toward England,
And cited up a thousand heavy times,
During the warres of Yorke and Lancaster
That had befalne us.   As we pac'd along
Upon the giddy footing of the Hatches,
Me thought that Glouster stumbled, and in falling
Strooke me (that thought to stay him) over-boord,
Into the tumbling billowes of the maine.
O Lord, me thought what paine it was to drowne,
What dreadfull noise of water in mine eares,
What sights of ugly death within mine eyes.
Me thoughts, I saw a thousand fearfull wrackes:
A thousand men that Fishes gnaw'd upon:
Wedges of Gold, great Anchors, heapes of Pearle,
Inestimable Stones, unvalewed Jewels,
All scattred in the bottome of the Sea,
Some lay in dead-mens Sculles, and in the holes
Where eyes did once inhabit, there were crept

(As 'twere in scorne of eyes) reflecting Gemmes,
That woo'd the slimy bottome of the deepe,
And mock'd the dead bones that lay scattred by.

FIRST FOLIO VERSE NOTES:

The punctuation works well for performance, even when it seems unnatural: **See Note 4**.

There are long thoughts ending in mid-line: **See Notes 2 & 18**.

The word 'thought' crops up in one form or another 5 times: **See Note 13**.

The rich description of drowning must indicate his real attitude, not the one it would be assumed he should have: **See Note 21**.

The line is spoken by the Keeper.

Editors change 'There we look'd' to 'Thence we look'd'.

'wrackes' = wrecks.

The Tragedy of Richard the Third, IV-2

TYRREL

The tyrannous and bloodie Act is done,
The most arch deed of pittious massacre
That ever yet this Land was guilty of:
Dighton and *Forrest*, who I did suborne
To do this peece of ruthfull Butchery,
Albeit they were flesht Villaines, bloody Dogges,
Melted with tendernesse, and milde compassion,
Wept like to Children, in their deaths sad Story.
O thus (quoth *Dighton*) lay the gentle Babes:
Thus, thus (quoth *Forrest*) girdling one another
Within their Alablaster innocent Armes:
Their lips were foure red Roses on a stalke,
And in their Summer Beauty kist each other.
A Booke of Prayers on their pillow lay,
Which one (quoth *Forrest*) almost chang'd my minde:
But oh the Divell, there the Villaine stopt:
When *Dighton* thus told on, we smothered
The most replenished sweet worke of Nature,
That from the prime Creation ere she framed.
Hence both are gone with Conscience and Remorse,
They could not speake, and so I left them both,
To beare this tydings to the bloody King.

FIRST FOLIO VERSE NOTES:

This is a perfect example of where a soliloquy is not 'the character's innermost thoughts', but a description of an act to enlighten the audience: **See Note 25**.

The speech starts and ends with 'bloody': **See Note 23**.

The first 8 lines are one thought leading to 'deaths sad Story': **See Note 2**.

'smothered' is both the end word in the line, and also (because of the '-ed' ending) pronounced in 3 syllables: **See Notes 7 & 9**.

The capitals are heavily used, and so an indication to the way the speech should be done: **See Note 5**.

The end of the speech is more factual than the beginning, and gives a shape to how it can be performed: **See Note 21**.

Editors change 'ruthfull Butchery' to 'ruthless Butchery'; 'milde compassion' to 'kind compassion'; 'like to Children' to 'like two Children'; and 'Which one (quoth *Forrest*)' to 'Which once (quoth *Forrest*)'.

The Shakespearean Verse Acting Check List

An approach to acting Shakespearean text; work through the following points in order:

A. Identify whether the piece is in prose or poetry — and make the appropriate acting conclusions — especially if you go from one to the other in a scene or part.

B. Remember: the passion is in the PUNCTUATION! The whole thought continues until the first *full stop* (or, in North American, the first *period*): [**.**]. Sometimes (if the next word begins with a Capital) the end of a thought is a *question mark*: [**?**], or an *exclamation mark*: [**!**]. If the thought is complicated, it may be made up of several sentences, joined together with *colons*: [**:**], or *semi-colons*: [**;**]. These are *less* than a full stop, and are *not* the end of the thought. A *colon* is similar to the words: 'therefore', or: 'because'; while a *semi-colon* is similar to: 'and'. A *colon* can sometimes be where a thought is broken, where the speaker's thoughts go off in another direction.

C. *Before* looking at the speech for the very first time, *highlight* the three words leading up to the end of a thought, so that you have the correct lengths of thought the very first time you read the speech. Often these words are what that particular thought is all about — so go through the speech just reading them out, to get a pattern for the whole speech. Notice where a thought ends in the middle of a line (a mid-line ending) and make sure you *do* something about this — *why* does your character want/need to come in with the next thought so quickly?

D. Go through the speech, reading aloud all the words that are in Capitals that are not at the start of a line — this will give you a series of stepping stones that again will help to show a pattern for the whole speech.

E. Notice what title you give to the person you are speaking to, whether it is 'thee' or 'you' (and if it changes in the speech); whether you address them in a consistent way, or whether it changes within the speech — and so shows a changing attitude.

F. Saying it out loud, find the masculine and feminine endings (and the Alexandrines!) and so choose the final word in each verse line or not, as appropriate.

G. By saying it out loud, find the verbal conceits: that is, the rhymes, alliterations, assonances, and repeated words. These help you to decide which words to choose. Remember, to choose is not simply to emphasise — choice *can* be by emphasis, but it can also be done with de-emphasis, changes in pitch or tone, or by pausing. These individual choices are up to the performer to decide — and the best way to do *that* is to rely on instinct — to do what you *feel*. This also applies to words you don't understand — what does their sound make you *feel*?

H. Saying it out loud, choose the similes, metaphors, the strange words, and words with double meanings – especially the bawdy ones.

I. Saying it out loud, find the rhythm breaks and changes, the full or half lines, and see what they are telling you, where you pause for business (never just a pause). Remember, a half-line at the start or finish of a speech is generally not a pause, but a note to join on with other speeches.

J. By doing all the above, and making all those choices, find the changing attitudes. Particularly notice when the language changes from simple to complex, and vice versa, as indications where the character is being straight forward, or not. (Saying complicated and witty lines 'sincerely' merely means doing them *untruthfully* and *badly*.)

K. *All* clues are there not just to be identified, but to inspire an acting choice — the audience cannot see inside your mind, so if they do not get it — forget it! More is more — three words alliterating is a bigger clue than two; repeating the same word seven times in a speech is a bigger clue than five times. Bigger clues need larger theatricalizations!

L. By doing all the above with the changing attitudes, find the character by making all these words and choices your own. *In other words, find the acting reason for your character to say these lines in this way and at this time.*

M. Finally, speed it all up – amazingly. THIS is what makes it take off and fly — *without* having to tone down the verse work to make it 'real' or 'sincere' — and then the words will start acting YOU.

First Line Index

The line in brackets indicates either a famous line in the body of the speech, or that the speech actually starts with this other line.

Remember that in Elizabethan printing, the letter 'I' can stand either for first person singular (I), or for Aye (yes). I have not chosen which: that is your — the performer's — job to decide which is the appropriate choice. After 1603, there came an injunction not to use the Lord's name in vain, so that in the First Folio occasionally the word 'Heaven' is substituted for 'God'. Again, I have left this as in the Folio.